Author's Note

When the proposal for *Crossing the Chasm* was under negotiation, both the publisher and the author agreed that if the book sold more than 5,000 copies, it would have done well. After all, it was a niche book from an unknown author addressed to the somewhat esoteric challenges of marketing high-tech products.

In fact, the book has sold over 300,000 copies since its first publication. Of course, publisher and author are delighted. But the more interesting question might be why the book was so successful. The answer is a textbook example of the effectiveness of word-of-mouth marketing, the very practice that the book advocates in its niche approach to gaining mainstream adoption for disruptive innovations.

First of all, it turned out that the metaphor of the chasm and the recommendations for how to cross it struck a deep chord among experienced high-tech managers. Countless readers have told me that, although they valued the material in the book, it really didn't tell them anything they didn't know already. Rather it captured what had been for them scattered intuitions and rueful learnings and put them into a coherent set of frameworks that could be used for future decision making.

This, in turn, caused them to pass the book along to colleagues, as much to spread the vocabulary as anything else. Thus the book left the marketing department and began to find its way to the engineering section, where a whole lot of readers claimed it was the first marketing book they didn't throw away after reading the early chapters. Praise from engineers is praise indeed, and the author was deeply grateful for this response.

This unusual turn of events also caught the eye of the venture capital community, which became a channel for more book sales. Venture capitalists saw in the new vocabulary a means to begin a market development dialogue with their engineering-oriented entrepreneurs. Indeed for whole companies the book became required reading, just to get everyone on the same page.

Professors at business schools then picked it up for their courses in entrepreneurial marketing, which was becoming all the rage in the years after the book's first release. Students liked the book because it is both descriptive and prescriptive in clear terms, largely because it communicates the core of its arguments through metaphors, mixed though they often may be. If you bought into the analogies, you pretty much had the essence of the book, and reading it was just a confirmation of what you already knew.

And so things went swimmingly until around 1997 or so when students began asking, "Who is Ashton Tate or Cullinet? What is Wordstar or Ingres?" The examples, which are key to any argument by analogy, had grown long in the tooth. And so a revised edition was published, keeping the arguments largely intact but substituting 1990s companies for their 1980s predecessors, further affirming the author's belief that chasms are a perennial feature of the tech sector's landscape.

And that brings us to today. In addition to a revised edition, the book has spawned two sequels of sorts: *Inside the Tornado,* which covers the opposite of the chasm challenge—how to market during hypergrowth—and *Living on the Fault Line,* which addresses how incumbent market leaders must respond to the next generation of technology challenges. It also created a platform for a fourth book, *The Gorilla Game,* coauthored with Paul Johnson and Tom Kippola, about how these same dynamics play out in stock market valuations for technology companies. And now in 2002, HarperCollins will be releasing the first wholly non-Moore entry into the chasm fray, *The Chasm Companion,* by my colleague Paul Wiefels.

In short, chasm writing and reading has become a cottage industry of sorts, and the technology sector has demonstrated extensive patience in absorbing its unending slew of metaphors from bowling alleys, tornadoes, and Main Street to gorillas, chimps, kings, and serfs, to GAP, CAP, core, and context, to who knows what next. All the author can say to this is that he tries to find whatever words can best capture the dynamics of the real-life situations his clients find themselves in.

And that leads to a final thought. Books are a collaboration between author and editor, and I am afraid I have worn out several in this journey, beginning with Virginia Smith, who championed *Crossing the Chasm* way back when, and subsequently including Kirsten Sandberg and now Dave Conti. HarperCollins and David continue to bear with me, and I with them, so the real question is how long the reading public will bear with the combination. I hope it will be for a long time to come.

Geoffrey Moore
April 2002

CROSSING THE CHASM

Marketing and Selling Disruptive Products to Mainstream Customers

Revised Edition

Geoffrey A. Moore

with a foreword by Regis McKenna

Collins Business *Essentials*
A Collins Business Book
An Imprint of HarperCollins Publishers

HarperCollins books may be purchased for educational, business, or sales promotional use. For information please write: Special Markets Department, HarperCollins Publishers, 10 East 53rd Street, New York, NY 10022.

The original hardcover of this book was published in 1991 by HarperBusiness, an Imprint of HarperCollins Publishers.

First Collins Business Essentials edition 2006.

The Library of Congress has catalogued a previous edition as follows:

Moore, Geoffrey A., 1946–
Crossing the chasm : marketing and selling high-tech products to mainstream customers / Geoffrey A. Moore.—Rev. ed.
p. cm.
Includes index.
ISBN 0-06662-002-3
1. Selling—High technology. 2. High technology—Marketing.
3. Technological immovations—Marketing. I. Title.
HF5439.H54M66   1999
658.8—dc21   98-55078

ISBN-10: 0-06-051712-3 (pbk.)
ISBN-13: 978-0-06-051712-0 (pbk.)

10 11 12 ❖/RRD 30 29 28 27 26 25

*To
Marie*

Contents

PART I

Discovering the Chasm

PART II

Crossing the Chasm

Preface to the Revised Edition

"Obiwan Kenobi," says Sir Alec Guinness in the original *Star Wars* movie—"Now there's a name I haven't heard for a long, long time."

The same might well be said of a number of the companies that served as examples in the original edition of *Crossing the Chasm*. Reading through its index brings to mind the medieval lament, "Where are the snows of yesteryear?" Where indeed are Aldus, Apollo, Ashton-Tate, Ask, Burroughs, Businessland, and the Byte Shop? Where are Wang, Weitek, and Zilog? "Oh lost and by the wind-grieved ghosts, come back again!"

But we should not despair. In high tech, the good news is that, although we lose our companies with alarming frequency, we keep the people along with the ideas, and so the industry as a whole goes forward vibrantly, even as the names on our paychecks slide into another seamlessly (OK, as seamlessly as our systems interoperate, which as marketing claims is . . . well that's another matter).

Crossing the Chasm was written in 1990 and published in 1991. Originally forecast to sell 5,000 copies, it has over a seven year period in the market sold more than 175,000. In high-tech marketing, we call this an "upside miss." The appeal of the book, I believe, is that it puts a vocabulary to a market development problem that has given untold grief to any number of high-tech enterprises. Seeing the problem externalized in print has a sort of redemptive effect on people who have fallen prey to it in the past—it wasn't all my fault! Moreover, like a good book on golf, its prescriptions give great hope that just by making this or that minor adjustment perfect results are bound to follow—this time we'll make it work! And so any number of people cheerfully have told me that the book has become the Bible in their company. So much for the spiritual health of our generation.

In editing this revised edition, I have tried to touch as little as possible the logic of the original. This is harder than you might think because over the past decade my views have changed (all right, I've become older), and I have an inveterate tendency to meddle, as any number of my clients and colleagues will testify. The problem is, when you meddle, you get in deeper and deeper until God knows what you have, but it wasn't what you started with. I have plenty enough opportunity to do that with future books, and I have enough respect for this one to try to stand off a bit.

That being said, I did make a few significant exceptions. I eliminated the section on using "thematic niches" as a legitimate tactic for crossing the chasm. It turns out instead they were a placeholder for the market tactics used during a merging hypergrowth market, a challenge covered in a subsequent book, *Inside the Tornado*. Also I have substituted a revised scenario process for the original to incorporate improvements that have evolved over the past several years of consulting at The Chasm Group. Elsewhere, I took a slightly new angle on creating the competition and, when it came to the section on distribution, I have done my best to incorporate the emerging influence of the Internet.

But the overwhelming bulk of the changes in this new edition—representing about a third of total text—simply swap out the original examples from the 1980s with new ones from the 1990s. Surprisingly, in the majority of cases this swap works very well. But in other cases, there's been a little force-fitting, and I want to beg your indulgence up front. The world has changed. The high-tech community is now crossing the chasm intentionally rather than unintentionally, and there are now competitors who have read the same book and create plans to block chasm-crossing. The basic forces don't change, but the tactics have become more complicated.

Moreover, we are seeing a new effect which was just barely visible in the prior decade, the piggybacking of one company's offer on another to skip the chasm entirely and jump straight into hypergrowth. In the 1980s Lotus piggybacked on VisiCalc to accomplish this feat in the spreadsheet category. In the 1990s Microsoft has done the same thing to Netscape in browsers. The key insight here is that we should always be tracking the evolution of a technology rather than a given company's product line—it's the Technology Adoption Life Cycle, after all. Thus it is spreadsheets, not VisiCalc, Lotus, or Excel, that is the adoption category, just as it is browsers, not Navigator or Explorer. In the early days products and categories were synonymous because technologies were on their first cycles. But today we have multiple decades of invention to build on, and a new offer is no longer quite as new or unprecedented as it used to be. The marketplace is therefore able to absorb this not-quite-so-new technology in gulps, for a while letting one company come to the fore, but substituting another should the first company stumble.

Finally, let me close by noting technological changes do not live in isolation but rather come under the influence of changes in surrounding technologies as well. In the early 90s it was the sea change to graphical user interfaces and client-server topologies that created the primary context. As we come to the close of the century it is the complete shift of communications infrastructure to the Internet. These major technology shifts create huge sine waves of change that interact with the smaller sine waves of more local technology shifts, occasionally synthesizing harmonically, more frequently playing out some discordant mix that has customers growling and investors howling.

Navigating in such uncharted waters requires beacons that can be seen above the waves, and that is what models in general, and the chasm models in particular, are for. Models are like constellations—they are not intended to change in themselves, but their value is in giving perspective on a highly changing world. The chasm model represents a pattern in market development that is based on the tendency of pragmatic people to adopt new technology when they see other people like them doing the same. This causes them to hang together as a group, and the group's initial reaction, like teenagers at a junior high dance, is to hesitate and watch. This is the chasm effect. The tendency is very deep-rooted, and so the pattern is very persistent. As a result, marketers can predict its appearance and build strategies to cope with it, and it is the purpose of this book to help in that process.

But fixing your position relative to the North Star does not keep water out of the boat. As the French proverb says, "God loves a sailor, but he has to row for himself." And in that act of rowing the work is huge and the risks high, and every reader of this book who is also a practitioner of high-tech market development has my deepest respect.

With that thought in mind, let me turn you over now to Regis McKenna, author of the original Foreword back in 1991, and then to a fledgling author writing his first acknowledgments.

Foreword

Within an ever-changing society, marketing represents the ongoing effort to keep the means of production—our products and services—in touch with evolving social and personal conditions. That "keeping in touch" has become our greatest challenge.

In an era when the pace of change was slower, the variety of products and services fewer, the channels of communication and distribution less pervasive, and the consumer less sophisticated, marketing could enjoy prolonged periods of relative stability, reaping profits from "holding the customer constant" and optimizing the other variables. That is no longer the case.

We live in an age of choice. We are continually bombarded with purchasing alternatives in every aspect of our lives. This in turn has led us to develop an increasingly sophisticated set of defenses, so that any company seeking to establish a "brand loyalty" in us is going to be hard-pressed to succeed. We demand more and more from our purchases and our suppliers, leading to increasingly fragmented markets served by products that can be customized by design, programmability, service, or variety.

There is a wonderful analogy to all this in the world of high technology. Behind the astounding proliferation of electronic systems, infiltrating our entertainment centers, our phones, our cares, and our kitchens, lies a technology called *application-specific integrated circuits,* or ASICs. These are tiny microprocessors that are producible in high volume up to the last layer, which is then designed *by the customers* to add the final veneer of personality needed for their specific product. ASICs embody many of the fundamental elements of modern marketing—radical customizability overlaid onto a constant and reliable foundation, dramatically shortened times to market, relatively small production runs, and an intense focus on customer service. They exemplify the remaking of our means of production to accommodate our changing social and personal needs.

As uplifting as all of this sounds in theory, in practice it represents a great challenge not only to our economic institutions but to the human spirit itself. We may celebrate change and growth, but that does not make either one the less demanding or painful. Our emerging and evolving markets are demanding continual adaptation and renewal, not only in times of difficulty but on the heels of our greatest successes as well. Which of us would not prefer a little more time to savor that success, to reap a little longer what we cannot help but feel are our just rewards? It is only natural to cling to the past when the past represents so much of what we have strived to achieve.

This is the key to *Crossing the Chasm*. The chasm represents the gulf between two distinct marketplaces for technology products—the first, an early market dominated by early adopters and insiders who are quick to appreciate the nature and benefits of the new development, and the second a mainstream market representing "the rest of us," people who want the benefits of new technology but who do not want to "experience" it in all its gory details. The transition between these two markets is anything but smooth.

Indeed, what Geoff Moore has brought into focus is that, at the time when one has just achieved great initial success in launching a new technology product, creating what he calls early market wins, one must undertake an immense effort and radical transformation to make the transition into serving the mainstream market. This transition involves sloughing off familiar entrepreneurial marketing habits and taking up new ones that at first feel strangely counterintuitive. It is a demanding time at best, and I will leave the diagnosis of its ailments and the prescription of its remedies to the insightful chapters that follow.

If we step back from this chasm problem, we can see it as an instance of the larger problem of how the marketplace can cope with change in general. For both the customer and the vendor, continually changing products and services challenge their institution's ability to absorb and make use of the new elements. What can marketing do to buffer these shocks?

Fundamentally, marketing must refocus away from *selling*

product and toward *creating relationship.* Relationship buffers the shock of change. To be sure, the specific product or service provided remains the fundamental basis for economic exchange, but it must not be treated as the main event. There is simply too much change in this domain for anyone to tolerate over the long haul. Instead, we must direct our attention toward creating and maintaining an ongoing customer relationship, so that as things change and stir in our immediate field of activity, we can look up over the smoke and dust and see an abiding partner, willing to cooperate and adjust with us as we take on our day-to-day challenges. Marketing's first deliverable is that partnership.

This is what we mean when we talk about "owning a market." Customers do not like to be "owned," if that implies lack of choice or freedom. The open systems movement in high tech is a clear example of that. But they do like to be "owned" if what that means is a vendor taking ongoing responsibility for the success of their joint ventures. Ownership in this sense means abiding commitment and a strong sense of mutuality in the development of the marketplace. When customers encounter this kind of ownership, they tend to become fanatically loyal to their supplier, which in turn builds a stable economic base for profitability and growth.

How can marketing foster such relationships? That question has driven the development of Regis McKenna Inc. since its inception. We began in the 1970s in our work with Intel and Apple where we tried to set a new tone around the adoption of technology products, to capture the imagination of a marketplace whose attentions were directed elsewhere. Working with Intel, Apple, Genentech and many other new technology companies, it became clear that traditional marketing approaches would not work. Business schools in America were educating their students to the ways of consumer marketing, and these graduates assumed that marketing was generic. Advertising and brand awareness became synonymous with marketing.

In the 1980s intense competition, even within small niches, created a new environment. With everyone competing for the customer's attention, the customer became king and demanded more substance than image. Advertising, as a medium of communication, could not sustain the kind of relationship that was needed for ongoing success. Two reasons in particular stood out.

First, as Vance Packard, in *The Hidden Persuaders*, and others educated the American populace to the manipulativeness of advertising, its credibility as a means of communication deteriorated. This was an extremely serious loss when it came to high-tech purchase decisions, because of what IBM used to call the "FUD factor"—the fear, uncertainty, and doubt that can plague decision makers when confronted with such an unfamiliar set of products and services. Just when they most want to trust in the communication process, they are confronted with an ad that they believe may be leading them astray.

The second problem with advertising is that it is a one-way mechanism of communication. As the emphasis shifts more and more from selling product to creating relationship, the demand for a two-way means of communication increases. Companies do not get it right the first time. To pick two current market-leading examples, the first Macintosh and the first release of Windows simply were not right—both needed major overhauls before they could become the runaway successes they represent today. This was only possible by Apple and Microsoft keeping in close touch with their customers and the other participants that make up the PC marketplace.

The standard we tried to set at RMI was one of education not promotion, the goal being to communicate rather than to manipulate, the mechanism being dialogue, not monologue. The fundamental requirement for the ongoing, interoperability needed to sustain high tech is accurate and honest exchange of information. Your partners need it, your distribution channel needs it and must support it, and your customers demand it. People in the 1990s simply will not put up with noncredible channels of communication. They will take their business elsewhere.

At RMI we call the building of market relationships *market relations*. The fundamental basis of market relations is to build and manage relationships with all the members that make up a high-tech marketplace, not just the most visible ones. In particular, it means setting up formal and informal communications not only with customers, press, and analysts but also with hardware and software partners, distributors, dealers, VARs, systems and integrators, user groups, vertically oriented industry organizations, universities, standards bodies, and international partners. It means improving not only your external communications but also your internal exchange of information among the sales force, the product managers, strategic planners, customer service and support, engineering, manufacturing, and finance.

To facilitate such relationships implies a whole new kind of expertise from a consulting organization. In addition to maintaining its communications disciplines, it must also provide experienced counsel and leadership in making fundamental marketing decisions. Market entry, market segmentation, competitive analysis, positioning, distribution, pricing—all these are issues with which a successful marketing effort must come to grips. And so we again remade ourselves, adding to market relations a second practice—high-tech marketing consulting.

Today, our practices of marketing consulting and market relations together are tackling the fundamental challenge of the 1990s—helping multiple players in the marketplace build what we call "whole product" solutions to market needs. Whole products represent completely configured solutions. Today, unlike the early 1980s, no single vendor, not even an IBM, can unilaterally provide the whole products needed. A new level of cooperation and communication must be defined and implemented so that companies—not just products—can "interoperate" to create these solutions.

Crossing the Chasm reflects much of this emphasis. Moore is a senior member of the RMI staff and has become an integral contributor to the development of our practice. An ex-professor and teacher by trade, he does not shrink from taking the stage to evangelize a new agenda. Part of that agenda is to make original contributions to the marketing discipline, and as you will see in the coming chapters, Geoff has done just that. At the same time, as he himself is quick to acknowledge, his colleagues and his clients have made immense contributions as well, and he is to be commended for his efforts in integrating these components into this work.

Finally, I would just like to say that this work is going to make you think. And the best way to prepare yourself for the fast-paced, ever-changing competitive world of marketing is to prepare yourself to think. This book adds the dimension of creative thinking as a prelude to action. It will change the way you think about marketing. It will change the way you think about market relationships.

Regis McKenna

Acknowledgments

The book that follows represents two years of writing. It also represents my last 13 years of employment in one or another segment of high tech sales and marketing. And most importantly, it reflects the last four years I have spent as a consultant at Regis McKenna Inc. During this period I have worked with scores of colleagues, sat in on innumerable client meetings, and dealt with myriad marketing problems. These are the "stuff" out of which this book has come.

Prior to entering the world of high tech, I was an English professor. One of the things I learned during this more scholarly period in my life was the importance of evidence and the necessity to document its sources. It chagrins me to have to say, therefore, that there are no documented sources of evidence anywhere in the book that follows. Although I routinely cite numerous examples, I have no studies to back them up, no corroborating witnesses, nothing.

I mention this because I believe it is fundamental to the way in which lessons are transmitted in universities and the way they are transmitted in the workplace. All of the information I use in day-to-day consulting comes to me by way of word of mouth. The fundamental research process for any given subject is to "ask around." There are rarely any real facts to deal with—not regarding the really important issues, anyway. Some of the information may come from reading, but since the sources quoted in the articles are the same as those one talks to, there is no reason to believe that the printed word has any more credibility than the spoken one. There is, in other words, no hope of a definitive answer. One is committed instead to an ongoing process of update and revision, always in search of the explanation that gives the best fit.

Given that kind of world, the single most important variable becomes who you talk with. The greatest pleasure of my past four years at RMI has been the quality of people I have encountered as my colleagues and my clients. In the next few paragraphs I want to acknowledge some of them specifically by name, but I know that by so doing I am bound to commit more than one sin of omission. From those who are not mentioned but who should have been, I ask forgiveness in advance.

Several of my current colleagues have offered ongoing input and criticism of this effort in its various conversational and manuscript forms. These include Paul Hodges, Randy Nickel, Elizabeth Chaney, Ellen Hipschman, Rosemary Remacle, Page Alloo, Karen Kang, Karen Lippe, Greg Ruff, Chris Halliwell, Patty Burke, Joan Naidish, Sharon Colby, and Patrick Corman.

Other colleagues who have since moved on to other ventures also provided wisdom, examples, and support. These include Jennifer Jones, Lee James, Lynn Amato, Bob Pearson, Mary Jane Reiter, Nancy Blake, Wendy Grubow, Jean Murphy, John Fess, Kathy Lockton, Andy Rothman, Rick Redding, Jennifer Little, and Wink Grellis. Then there is that one colleague who has cheerfully provided her hard labor in the copying, mailing, faxing, phoning, coordinating and all else that goes into getting a book out. Thank you, Brete Wirth.

Clients and friends—not mutually exclusive groups, I am happy to say—have also been extremely supportive of this effort, both in critiquing drafts of the manuscript and in contributing to the ideas and examples. In this regard, I would especially like to acknowledge John Rizzo, Sam Darcie, David Taylor, Brett Bullington, Tom Quinn, Tom Loeb, Phil Vertin, Mike Whitfield, Bill Leavy, Ed Sterbenc, Bob Jolls, Bob Healy, Paul Wiefels, Mark and Chuck Dehner, Doug Edwards, Corinne Smith, John Zeisler, Jane Gaynor, Bob Lefkowits, Camillo Wilson, Ed Sattizahn, Jon Rant, John Oxaal, Isadore Katz, and Tony Zingale.

From the hoard of interesting remarks of independent consultants and occasional competitors, many of whom are also good friends, I have pillaged cheerfully whenever I could. These include Roberta Graves, Tony Morris, Sy Merrin, Kathy Lane, Leigh Marriner, Dick Shaffer, Esther Dyson, Jeff Tarter, and Stewart Alsop.

Then we come to that core group of friends whose importance

goes beyond specific contributions to this or that idea or chapter and lodges instead somewhere near support of the soul. These exceptionally special folk include Doug Molitor, Glenn Helton, Peter Schireson, Skye Hallberg, and Steve Flint.

Beyond that, there are three more people without whom this book would not be possible. The first of these is Regis McKenna, my boss, founder of my company and funder of my livelihood, and in many senses the inventor of the high-tech marketing practice I am now trying to extend. The second is Jim Levine, my literary agent, the man who took a look at 200-odd pages of manuscript a year or so ago and allowed as how, although it wasn't a book, it might have possibilities. And the third is Virginia Smith, my editor, who has been guiding me this past year through the bizarre intricacies of the book publishing business.

There remains one last group of people to name, those who have been at the center of almost anything I have ever undertaken: my parents, George and Patty; my brother, Peter; my children, Margaret, Michael, and Anna; and my wife, Marie. I am particularly indebted to Marie, for many reasons that go well beyond this book, but specifically in this instance for making the countless sacrifices and giving the kind of emotional and practical day-to-day support that make writing a book possible, and for being the kind of person that inspires me to undertake such challenges.

PART I

DISCOVERING
THE CHASM

Introduction

If Bill Gates Can
Be a Billionaire

There is a line from a song in the musical *A Chorus Line:* "If Troy Donahue can be a movie star, then I can be a movie star." Every year one imagines hearing a version of this line reprised in high-tech start-ups across the country: "If Bill Gates can be a billionaire . . ." For indeed, the great thing about high tech is that, despite numerous disappointments, it still holds out the siren's lure of a legitimate get-rich-quick opportunity.

But let us set our sights a little more modestly. Let us say, "If in the 1980s two guys, each named Mike Brown (one from Portland, Oregon, and the other from Lenexa, Kansas), can in 10 years found two companies no one has ever heard of (Central Point Software and Innovative Software), and bring to market two software products that have hardly become household names (PC Tools Deluxe and Smartware) and still be able to cash out in seven figures, then, by God, we should be able to too."

This is the great lure. And yet, as even the Bible has warned us, while many are called, few are chosen. Every year millions of dollars—not to mention countless work hours of our nation's best technical talent—are lost in failed attempts to join this kingdom of the elect. And oh what wailing then, what gnashing of teeth!

"Why me?" cries out the unsuccessful entrepreneur. Or rather, "Why *not* me?" "Why not us?" chorus his equally unsuccessful investors. "Look at our product. Is it not as good—nay, better—than the product that beat us out? How can you say that Oracle is better than Sybase, Microsoft Word is better than Word-Perfect, Cisco's routers are better than Bay Networks', or that Pentium is better than the Power PC?" How, indeed? For in fact, feature for feature, the less successful product is often arguably superior.

Not content to slink off the stage without some revenge, this sullen and resentful crew casts about among themselves to find a scapegoat, and whom do they light upon? With unfailing consistency and unerring accuracy, all fingers point to—*the vice-president of marketing*. It is marketing's fault! Oracle outmarketed Sybase, Microsoft outmarketed WordPerfect, Cisco outmarketed Bay, Intel outmarketed Motorola. Now we too have been outmarketed. Firing is too good for this monster. Hang him!

While this sort of thing takes its toll on the marketing profession, there is more at stake in these failures than a bumpy executive career path. When a high-tech venture fails everyone goes down with the ship—not only the investors but also the engineers, the manufacturers, the president, and the receptionist. All those extra hours worked in hopes of cashing in on an equity option—all gone.

Worse still, because there is no clear reason why one venture succeeds and the next one fails, the sources of capital to fund new products and companies become increasingly wary of investing. Interest rates go up, and the willingness to entertain venture risks goes down. Wall Street has long been at wit's end when it comes to high-tech stocks. Despite the efforts of some of its best analysts, these stocks are traditionally undervalued, and exceedingly volatile. It is not uncommon for a high-tech company to announce even a modest shortfall in its quarterly projections and incur a 20 to 30 percent devaluation in stock price on the following day of trading.

There is an even more serious ramification. High-tech inventiveness and marketing expertise are two cornerstones of the U.S. strategy for global competitiveness. We will never have the lowest cost of labor or raw materials, so we must continue to exploit advantages further down the value chain. If we cannot at least learn to predictably and successfully bring high-tech products to market, our counterattack will falter, placing our entire standard of living in jeopardy.

With so much at stake, the erratic results of high-tech marketing are particularly frustrating, especially in a society where other forms of marketing appear to be so well under control. Elsewhere—in cars or TVs or microwaves—we may see ourselves being outmanufactured, but not outmarketed. Indeed, even after we have lost an entire category of goods to offshore competition, we remain the experts in marketing these goods to U.S. consumers. Why haven't we been able to apply these same skills to high tech? And what is it going to take for us to finally get it right?

It is the purpose of this book to answer these two questions in considerable detail. But the short answer is as follows: Our current model for how to develop a high-tech market is almost—but not quite—right. As a result, our marketing ventures, despite normally promising starts, drift off course in puzzling ways, eventually causing unexpected and unnerving gaps in sales revenues, and sooner or later leading management to undertake some desperate remedy. Occasionally these remedies work out, and the result is a high-tech marketing success. (Of course, when these are written up in retrospect, what was learned in hindsight is not infrequently portrayed as foresight, with the result that no one sees how perilously close to the edge the enterprise veered.) More often, however, the remedies either flat-out fail, and a product or a company goes belly up, or they progress after a fashion to some kind of limp but breathing half-life, in which the company has long since abandoned its dreams of success and contents itself with once again making payroll.

None of this is necessary. We have enough high-tech marketing history now to see where our model has gone wrong and how to fix it. To be specific, the point of greatest peril in the development of a high-tech market lies in making the transition from an *early market* dominated by a few *visionary* customers to a *mainstream market* dominated by a large block of customers who are predominantly *pragmatists* in orientation. The gap between these two markets, heretofore ignored, is in fact so significant as to warrant being called a *chasm,* and crossing this chasm must be the primary focus of any long-term high-tech marketing plan. A successful crossing is how high-tech fortunes are made; failure in the attempt is how they are lost.

For the past decade and more, I, along with my colleagues at The Chasm Group, have watched countless companies struggle to maintain their footing during this difficult period. It is an extremely difficult transition for reasons that will be summarized in the opening chapters of the book. The good news is that there are reliable guiding principles. The material in this book was born of hundreds of consulting engagements focused on bringing products and companies into profitable and sustainable mainstream markets. The models presented here have been tested again and again and have been found effective. The chasm, in sum, can be crossed.

Like a hermit crab that has outgrown its shell, the company crossing the chasm must scurry to find its new home. Until it does, it will be prey to all kinds of predators. This urgency means that everyone in the company—not just the marketing and sales people—must focus all their efforts on this one end until it is accomplished. Chapters 3 through 7 set forth the principles necessary to guide high-tech ventures during this period of great risk. This section focuses on marketing, because that is where the leadership must come from, but I ultimately argue in the Conclusion that leaving the chasm behind requires significant changes throughout the high-tech enterprise. The book closes, therefore, with a call for new strategies in the areas of finance, organizational development, and R&D.

This book is unabashedly about and for marketing within high-tech enterprises. But high tech can be viewed as a microcosm of larger industrial trends. In particular, the relationship between an early market and a mainstream market is not unlike the relationship between a fad and a trend. Marketing has long known how to exploit fads and how to develop trends. The problem, since these techniques are antithetical to each other, is that you need to decide which one—fad or trend—you are dealing with before you start. It would be much better if you could start with a fad, exploit it for all it was worth, and then turn it into a trend.

That may seem like a miracle, but that is in essence what high-tech marketing is all about. Every truly innovative high-tech product starts out as a fad—something with no known market value or purpose but with "great properties" that generate a lot of enthusiasm within an "in crowd." That's the early market.

Then comes a period during which the rest of the world watches to see if anything can be made of this; that is the chasm. If in fact something does come out of it—if a value proposition is discovered that can predictably be delivered to a targetable set of customers at a reasonable price—then a new mainstream market forms, typically with a rapidity that allows its initial leaders to become very, very successful.

The key in all this is crossing the chasm—making that mainstream market emerge. This is a do-or-die proposition for high-tech enterprises; hence, it is logical that they be the crucible in which "chasm theory" is formed. But the principles can be generalized to other forms of marketing, so for the general reader who can bear with all the high-tech examples in this book, useful lessons may be learned.

One of the most important lessons about crossing the chasm is that the task ultimately requires achieving an unusual degree of company unity during the crossing period. This is a time when one should forgo the quest for eccentric marketing genius, in favor of achieving an informed consensus among mere mortals. It is a time not for dashing and expensive gestures but rather for careful plans and cautiously rationed resources—a time not to gamble all on some brilliant coup but rather to focus everyone on making as few mistakes as possible.

One of the functions of this book, therefore—and perhaps its most important one—is to open up the logic of marketing decision making during this period so that everyone on the management team can participate in the marketing process. If prudence rather than brilliance is to be our guiding principle, then many heads are better than one. If marketing is going to be the driving force—and most organizations insist this is their goal—then its principles must be accessible to all the players, and not, as is sometimes the case, be reserved to an elect few who have managed to penetrate its mysteries.

Crossing the Chasm, therefore, is written for the entire high-tech community—for everyone who is a stakeholder in the venture, engineers as well as marketeers, and financiers as well. All must come to a common accord if the chasm is to be safely negotiated. And with that thought in mind, let us turn to Chapter 1.

1

High-Tech Marketing Illusion

As the revised edition of this book is being written, it is 1998, and for this time we have seen a commercial release of the electric car. General Motors makes one, and Ford and Chrysler are sure to follow. Let's assume the cars work like any other, except they are quieter and better for the environment. Now the question is: When are you going to buy one?

The Technology Adoption Life Cycle

Your answer to the preceding question will tell a lot about how you relate to the *Technology Adoption Life Cycle*, a model for understanding the acceptance of new products. If your answer is, "Not until hell freezes over," you are probably a very late adopter of technology, what we call in the model a *laggard*. If your answer is, "When I have seen electric cars prove themselves and when there are enough service stations on the road," you might be a middle-of-the-road adopter, or in the model, the *early majority*. If you say, "Not until most people have made the switch and it becomes really inconvenient to drive a gasoline car," you are probably more of a follower, a member of the *late majority*. If, on the other hand, you want to be the first one on your block with an electric car, you are apt to be an *innovator* or an *early adopter*.

In a moment we are going to take a look at these labels in greater detail, but first we need to understand their significance. It turns out our attitude toward technology adoption becomes significant—at least in a marketing sense—any time we are introduced to products that require us to change our current mode of behavior or to modify other products and services we rely on. In academic terms, such change-sensitive products are called *discontinuous innovations*. The contrasting term, *continuous innovations*, refers to the normal upgrading of products that does not require us to change behavior.

For example, when Crest promises you whiter teeth, that is a continuous innovation. You still are brushing the same teeth in the same way with the same toothbrush. When Ford's new Taurus promises better mileage, when Dell's latest computer promises faster processing times and more storage space, or when Sony promises sharper and brighter TV pictures, these are all continuous innovations. As a consumer, you don't have to change your ways in order to take advantage of these improvements.

On the other hand, if the Sony were a high-definition TV, it would be incompatible with today's broadcasting standards, which would require you to seek out special sources of programming. This would be a discontinuous innovation because you would have to change your normal TV-viewing behavior. Similarly if the new Dell computer were to come with the Be operating system, it would be incompatible with today's software base. Again, you would be required to seek out a whole new set of software, thereby classifying this too as a discontinuous innovation. Or if the new Ford car, as we just noted, required electricity instead of gasoline, or if the new toothpaste were a mouthwash that did not use a toothbrush, then once again you would have a product incompatible with your current infrastructure of supporting components. In all these cases, the innovation demands significant changes by not only the consumer but also the infrastructure. That is how and why such innovations come to be called discontinuous.

Between *continuous* and *discontinuous* lies a spectrum of demands for change. TV dinners, unlike microwave dinners, did not require the purchase of a new oven, but they did require the purchase of more freezer space. Color-TV programming did not, like VCRs, require investing in and mastering a new technology, but they did require buying a new TV and learning more about tuning and antennas than many of us wanted to learn. The special washing instructions for certain fabrics, the special street lanes reserved for bicycle riders, the special dialing instructions for calling overseas—all represent some new level of demand on the consumer to absorb a change in behavior. Sooner or later, all businesses must make these demands. And so it is that all businesses can profit by lessons from high-tech industries.

Whereas other industries introduce discontinuous innovations only occasionally and with much trepidation, high-tech enterprises do so routinely and as confidently as a born-again Christian holding four aces. From their inception, therefore, high-tech industries needed a marketing model that coped effectively with this type of product introduction. Thus the Technology Adoption Life Cycle became central to the entire sector's approach to marketing. (People are usually amused to learn that the original research that gave rise to this model was done on the adoption of new strains of seed potatoes among American farmers. Despite these agrarian roots, however, the model has thoroughly transplanted itself into the soil of Silicon Valley.)

The model describes the market penetration of any new technology product in terms of a progression in the types of consumers it attracts throughout its useful life:

As you can see, we have a bell curve. The divisions in the curve are roughly equivalent to where standard deviations would fall. That is, the early majority and the late majority fall within one standard deviation of the mean, the early adopters and the laggards within two, and way out there, at the very onset of a new technology, about three standard deviations from the norm, are the innovators.

The groups are distinguished from each other by their characteristic response to a discontinuous innovation based on a new technology. Each group represents a unique *psychographic* profile—a combination of psychology and demographics that makes its marketing responses different from those of the other groups. Understanding each profile and its relationship to its neighbors is a critical component of high-tech marketing lore.

Technology Adoption Life Cycle

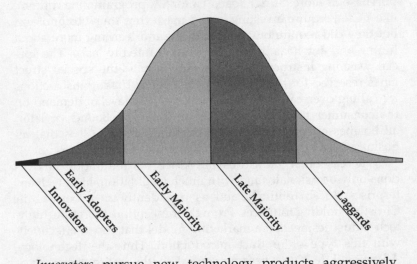

Innovators   Early Adopters   Early Majority   Late Majority   Laggards

Innovators pursue new technology products aggressively. They sometimes seek them out even before a formal marketing program has been launched. This is because technology is a central interest in their life, regardless of what function it is performing. At root they are intrigued with any fundamental advance and often make a technology purchase simply for the pleasure of exploring the new device's properties. There are not very many innovators in any given market segment, but winning them over at the outset of a marketing campaign is key nonetheless, because their endorsement reassures the other players in the marketplace that the product does in fact work.

Early adopters, like innovators, buy into new product concepts very early in their life cycle, but unlike innovators, they are not technologists. Rather they are people who find it easy to imagine, understand, and appreciate the benefits of a new technology, and to relate these potential benefits to their other concerns. Whenever they find a strong match, early adopters are willing to base their buying decisions upon it. Because early adopters do not rely on well-established references in making these buying decisions, preferring instead to rely on their own intuition and vision, they are key to opening up any high-tech market segment.

The early majority share some of the early adopter's ability to relate to technology, but ultimately they are driven by a strong sense of practicality. They know that many of these newfangled inventions end up as passing fads, so they are content to wait and see how other people are making out before they buy in themselves. They want to see well-established references before investing substantially. Because there are so many people in this segment—roughly one-third of the whole adoption life cycle—winning their business is key to any substantial profits and growth.

The *late majority* shares all the concerns of the early majority, plus one major additional one: Whereas people in the early majority are comfortable with their ability to handle a technology product, should they finally decide to purchase it, members of the late majority are not. As a result, they wait until something has become an established standard, and even then they want to see lots of support and tend to buy, therefore, from large, well-established companies. Like the early majority, this group comprises about one-third of the total buying population in any given segment. Courting its favor is highly profitable indeed, for while profit margins decrease as the products mature, so do the selling costs, and virtually all the R&D costs have been amortized.

Finally there are the *laggards*. These people simply don't want anything to do with new technology, for any of a variety of reasons, some personal and some economic. The only time they ever buy a technological product is when it is buried so deep inside another product—the way, say, that a microprocessor is designed into the braking system of a new car—that they don't even know it is there. Laggards are generally regarded as not worth pursuing on any other basis.

To recap the logic of the Technology Adoption Life Cycle, its underlying thesis is that technology is absorbed into any given community in stages corresponding to the psychological and social profiles of various segments within that community. This process can be thought of as a continuum with definable stages, each associated with a definable group, and each group making up a predictable portion of the whole.

The High-Tech Marketing Model

This profile, is in turn, the very foundation of the High-Tech Marketing Model. That model says that the way to develop a high-tech market is to work the curve left to right, focusing first on the innovators, growing that market, then moving on to the early adopters, growing that market, and so on, to the early majority, late majority, and even to the laggards. In this effort, companies must use each "captured" group as a reference base for going on to market to the next group. Thus, the endorsement of innovators becomes an important tool for developing a credible pitch to the early adopters, that of the early adopters to the early majority, and so on.

The idea is to keep this process moving smoothly, proceeding something like passing the baton in a relay race or imitating Tarzan swinging from vine to well-placed vine. It is important to maintain momentum in order to create a bandwagon effect that makes it natural for the next group to want to buy in. Too much of a delay and the effect would be something like hanging from a motionless vine—nowhere to go but down. (Actually, going down is the graceful alternative. What happens more often is a desperate attempt to re-create momentum, typically through some highly visible form of promotion, which ends up making the company look like a Tarzan frantically jerking back and forth, trying to get a vine moving with no leverage. This typically leads the other animals in the jungle just to sit and wait for him to fall.)

There is an additional motive for maintaining momentum: to keep ahead of the next emerging technology. Portable electric typewriters were displaced by portable PCs, which in turn may someday be displaced by Internet terminals. You need to take advantage of your day in the sun before the next day renders you obsolete. From this notion comes the idea of a *window of opportunity*. If momentum is lost, then we can be overtaken by a competitor, thereby losing the advantages exclusive to a technology leadership position—specifically, the profit-margin advantage during the middle to late stages, which is the primary source from which high-tech fortunes are made.

This, in essence, is the High-Tech Marketing Model—a vision of a smooth unfolding through all the stages of the Technology Adoption Life Cycle. What is dazzling about this concept, particularly to those who own equity in a high-tech venture, is its promise of virtual monopoly over a major new market development. If you can get there first, "catch the curve," and ride it up through the early majority segment, thereby establishing the de facto standard, you can get rich very quickly and "own" a highly profitable market for a very long time to come.

Testimonials

Lotus 1-2-3 is a prime example of optimizing the High-Tech Marketing Model. No one has ever argued that it was the best spreadsheet program ever written. Certainly it wasn't the first, and many of the features people appreciate about it most were in fact derived directly from VisiCalc, its predecessor that ran on the Apple II. But Lotus 1-2-3 was the first spreadsheet for the IBM PC, and its designers were careful to tune its performance specifically for that platform. As a result, the innovators liked Lotus 1-2-3 because it was slick and fast. Then the early adopters liked it because it allowed them to do something they had never been able to do before—what later became popularized as "what if" analysis. The early majority liked the spreadsheet because it fell into line with some very common business operations, like budgeting, sales forecasting, and project tracking. As more and more people began to use it, it became harder and harder to use anything else, including paper and pencil, so the late majority gradually fell into line. This was the tool people knew how to use. If you wanted to share a spreadsheet, it had to be in Lotus format. Thus it became so entrenched that by the end of the 1980s well over half the IBM PCs and PC compatibles with spreadsheets had Lotus 1-2-3—despite the fact that there were numerous competitors, many of which were, feature for feature, superior products.

Astounding as this accomplishment is, many other companies have achieved a comparable status. This is what Oracle has achieved in the area of relational databases, Microsoft in PC operating systems, Hewlett-Packard in PC laser and inkjet printers, and IBM in mainframe computers. It is the position that Netscape is clinging to in Internet browsers, Autodesk holds in PC CAD, ESRI has in GIS software, Cisco has in routers, and Intel has in microprocessors.

Each of these companies holds market share in excess of 50 percent in its prime market. All of them have been able to establish strongholds in the early majority segment, if not beyond, and to look forward from that position to continued growth, won-

drously strong profit margins, and increasingly preferred relationships as suppliers to their customers. To be sure, some like
Oracle and, more dramatically, Netscape have fallen on hard
times, but even then customers often bend over backwards to
give market share leaders second and third chances, bringing
cries of anguish from their competitors who would never be
granted such grace.

It should come as no surprise that the history of these flagship
products conforms to the High-Tech Marketing Model. In truth,
the model was essentially derived from an abstraction of these
histories. And so high-tech marketing, as we enter the next mil-
lennium, keeps before it the example of these companies and the
abstraction of the High-Tech Marketing Model, and marches confidently forward.

Of course, if that were a sufficient formula for success, you
would need to read no further.

Illusion and Disillusion:
Cracks in the Bell Curve

It is now time to advise you that there are any number of us in
Silicon Valley who are willing to testify that there is something
wrong with the High-Tech Marketing Model. We believe this to
be true because we all own what once were meaningful equity
stakes in corporations that either no longer exist or whose current
valuation is so diluted that our stock—were there a market for it,
which there is not—has lost all monetary significance.

Although we all experienced our fates uniquely, much of our
shared experience can be summarized by recasting the Technology Adoption Life Cycle in the following way:

As you can see, the components of the life cycle are un-
changed, but between any two psychographic groups has been
introduced a gap. This symbolizes the dissociation between the
two groups—that is, the difficulty any group will have in accept-
ing a new product if it is presented in the same way as it was to
the group to its immediate left. Each of these gaps represents an
opportunity for marketing to lose momentum, to miss the transition to the next segment, thereby never to gain the promised land
of profit-margin leadership in the middle of the bell curve.

The *Revised* Technology Adoption Life Cycle

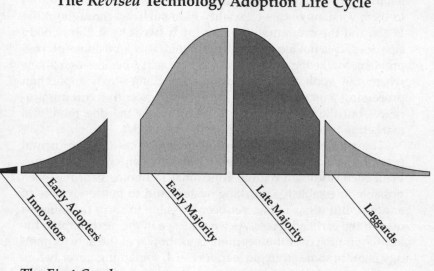

The First Crack

Two of the gaps in the High-Tech Marketing Model are relatively minor—what one might call "cracks in the bell curve"—yet even here unwary ventures have slipped and fallen. The first is between the innovators and the early adopters. It is a gap that occurs when a hot technology product cannot be readily translated into a major new benefit—something like Esperanto. The enthusiast loves it for its architecture, but nobody else can even figure out how to start using it.

At present, neural networking software falls into this category. Available since the 1980s, this software mimics the structure of the brain, actually programming itself through the use of feedback and rules to improve its performance against a given task. It is a terribly exciting technology because, for the first time, it holds out the possibility that computers can teach themselves and develop solutions that no human programmer could design from scratch. Nonetheless, the software has shown little commercial success because there has not yet emerged a unique and compelling application that would drive its acceptance over other, more established alternatives.

Another example of a product that fell through the crack between the innovators and the early adopters is desktop video conferencing. At numerous R&D labs from Xerox to Intel to PictureTel to IBM, versions of this capability have surfaced throughout the 1990s, and the inventors who develop it swear by it. But nobody else does. It is not a bandwidth problem. It is a business process problem. Marketing groups keep on forecasting business situations where the application would be compelling—loan application processing, customer service in general, executive communications—but the dogs keep on refusing to eat the dog food, and marketing teams keep getting, well, "recycled."

The market-development problem in the case of both neural networking software and desktop video conferencing is this: With each of these exciting, functional technologies it has been possible to establish a working system and to get innovators to adopt it. But it has not as yet been possible to carry that success over to the early adopters. As we shall see in the next chapter, the key to winning over this segment is to show that the new technology enables some strategic leap forward, something never before possible, which has an intrinsic value and appeal to the nontechnologist. This benefit is typically symbolized by a single, compelling application, the one thing that best captures the power and value of the new product. If the marketing effort is unable to find that compelling application, then market development stalls with the innovators, and the future of the product falls through the crack.

The Other Crack

There is another crack in the bell curve, of approximately equal magnitude, that falls between the early majority and the late majority. By this point in the Technology Adoption Life Cycle, the market is already well developed, and the technology product has been absorbed into the mainstream. The key issue now, transitioning from the early to the late majority, has to do with demands on the end user to be technologically competent.

Simply put, the early majority is willing and able to become technologically competent, where necessary; the late majority, much less so. When a product reaches this point in the market development, it must be made increasingly easier to adopt in order to continue being successful. If this does not occur, the transition to the late majority may well stall or never happen.

Programmable VCRs are currently in this situation, as are high-end office copier systems, and a whole slew of telephones which offer call forwarding, three-way conferencing, or even just call transferring. How many times have you been on the phone and heard—or said—"Now I may lose you when I hit the transfer button, so be sure to call back if I do." The problem is that for people who are not frequent users of the system the protocols are simply too hard to remember. As a result, users do not use the features, and so companies in mature markets find it harder and harder to get paid for the R&D they have done because the end user cannot capture the benefit. Instead, they bemoan that the product has become a commodity when in fact it is the *experience* of the product that has been commoditized. This truly is marketing's fault, particularly when companies have ceded marketing the right to redesign the user interface and thus control the user experience.

Other examples of products in danger of falling through the crack between the early and late majority are scanners for adding images to PC presentations and desktop publishing software. The market leaders in these two areas, Hewlett-Packard and Adobe respectively, have been quite successful in capturing the early majority, but their products still give conservatives in the late majority pause. And so these categories are in danger of stagnating although neither market is in fact saturated.

Discovering the Chasm

The real news, however, is not the two cracks in the bell curve, the one between the innovators and the early adopters, the other between the early and late majority. No, the real news is the deep and dividing *chasm* that separates the early adopters from the early majority. This is by far the most formidable and unforgiving transition in the Technology Adoption Life Cycle, and it is all the more dangerous because it typically goes unrecognized.

The reason the transition can go unnoticed is that with both groups the customer list and the size of the order can look the same. Typically, in either segment, you would see a list of Fortune 500 to Fortune 2000 customers making relatively large orders—five figures for sure, more often six figures or even higher.

But in fact the basis for the sale—what has been promised, implicitly or explicitly, and what must be delivered—is radically different.

What the early adopter is buying, as we shall see in greater detail in Chapter 2, is some kind of *change agent*. By being the first to implement this change in their industry, the early adopters expect to get a jump on the competition, whether from lower product costs, faster time to market, more complete customer service, or some other comparable business advantage. They expect a radical discontinuity between the old ways and the new, and they are prepared to champion this cause against entrenched resistance. Being the first, they also are prepared to bear with the inevitable bugs and glitches that accompany any innovation just coming to market.

By contrast, the early majority want to buy a *productivity improvement* for existing operations. They are looking to minimize the discontinuity with the old ways. They want evolution, not revolution. They want technology to enhance, not overthrow, the established ways of doing business. And above all, they do not want to debug somebody else's product. By the time they adopt it, they want it to work properly and to integrate appropriately with their existing technology base.

This contrast just scratches the surface relative to the differences and incompatibilities among early adopters and the early majority. Let me just make two key points for now: Because of these incompatibilities, early adopters do not make good references for the early majority. And because of the early majority's concern not to disrupt their organizations, good references are critical to their buying decisions. So what we have here is a catch-22. The only suitable reference for an early majority customer, it turns out, is another member of the early majority, but no upstanding member of the early majority will buy without first having consulted with several suitable references.

Bodies in the Chasm

What happens in this catch-22 situation? First, because the product *has* caught on with the early adopters, it has gotten a lot of publicity. In networking, consider gigabit Ethernet, optical switching, cable modems, and Digital Subscriber Loops; in PCs voice processing for dictation, interoperability with television, and specialized devices like the electronic book; in peripherals, personal digital assistants for email and Internet access, keyboards with built-in scanners, and "table-free" gyroscopic mice that operate in free space; in enterprise software, applications for data mining, target marketing and end-to-end supply chain visibility; and on the Internet itself, 3D worlds genned up of VRML, IP telephony, and following that, IP video conferencing. We have all read a lot about these types of products, yet not one has achieved to date a mainstream market leadership position, despite the fact that the products actually do work reasonably well. In large part this is because of the high degree of discontinuity implicit in their adoption by organizations, and the inability of the marketing effort, to date, to lower this barrier to the early majority. So the products languish, continuing to feed off the early adopter segment of the market, but unable to really take off and break through to the high-volume opportunities.

The classic example of this scenario for the 1990s was client-server computing for enterprise applications. In 1987 it was proclaimed by The Gartner Group as the enterprise architecture for the coming decade, and indeed every IT department genuflected in agreement. Every year thereafter there would be articles about breakthroughs in client-server hardware, the arrival of mission-critical RDBMS software, new tools for GUI front ends, but at the end of the day, all that sold was server-centric mainframe and minicomputer packages. It was not until 1992—five years into the making—that client-server finally emerged as a viable software category, and it wasn't until 1995—eight years later—that it finally overtook its server-centric ancestor.

Why so long? Client-server computing required, among other things, a standard client with GUI capabilities. In 1987 the standard client was a DOS computer. There were four graphical alternatives—Unix, Macintosh, OS/2, and Windows. The announced intent of IBM and Microsoft was to make OS/2 the replacement platform. But that floundered, and both Unix and Macintosh thrived, while Windows lagged—and so the whole market lagged until finally Windows 3.0 emerged as the new de facto standard. At that time PeopleSoft introduced its client-server package for Human Relations with Windows clients—and the market was launched.

Let's look at another example. One of the great cover stories of the early 1980s was artificial intelligence (AI)—brains in a box. Everybody was writing about it, and many prestigious customer organizations were jumping on the bandwagon of companies like Teknowledge, Symbolics, and Intellicorp. Indeed, the customer list of any one of these companies looked like a Who's Who of the Fortune 100. Early AI pioneers, like Tom Kehler, the chairman of Intellicorp, routinely got coverage everywhere from *Inc.* and *High Technology* to *Time* magazine to the front page of the *Wall Street Journal*, and among other things, were able to ride that wave of enthusiasm to take their companies public.

Today, however, AI has been relegated to the trash heap. Despite the fact that it was—and is—a very hot technology, and that it garnered strong support from the early adopters, who saw its potential for using computers to aid human decision making, it has simply never caught on as a product for the mainstream market. Why? When it came time for the early majority to absorb it into the mainstream, there were too many obstacles to its adoption: lack of support for mainstream hardware, inability to integrate it easily into existing systems, no established design methodology, and a lack of people trained in how to implement it. So AI languished at the entrance to the mainstream, for lack of a sustained marketing effort to lower the barriers to adoption, and after a while it got a reputation as a failed attempt. And as soon as that happened, the term itself became taboo.

So today, although the technology of AI is alive and kicking, underlying such currently popular manifestations as so-called expert systems and object-oriented programming, no one uses the phrase *artificial intelligence* in their marketing efforts. And a company like Intellicorp, which had struggled desperately to be profitable as an AI firm, has backed completely away from that identity.

In sum, when promoters of high-tech products try to make the transition from a market base made up of visionary early adopters to penetrate the next adoption segment, the pragmatist early majority, they are effectively operating *without a reference base and without a support base within a market that is highly reference oriented and highly support oriented.*

This is indeed a chasm, and into this chasm many an unwary start-up venture has fallen. Despite repeated instances of the chasm effect, however, high-tech marketing has yet to get this problem properly in focus. Indeed, that is the function of this book. As a final prelude to that effort, therefore, by way of evoking additional glimmers of recognition and understanding of this plight of the chasm, I offer the following parable as a kind of condensation of the entrepreneurial experience gone awry.

A High-Tech Parable

In the first year of selling a product—most of it alpha and beta release—the emerging high-tech company expands its customer list to include some technology enthusiast innovators and one or two visionary early adopters. Everyone is pleased, and at the first annual Christmas party, held on the company premises, plastic glasses and potluck canapés are held high.

In the second year—the first year of true product—the company wins over several more visionary early adopters, including a handful of truly major deals. Revenue meets plan, and everyone is convinced it is time to ramp up—especially the venture capitalists who note that next year's plan calls for a 300 percent increase in revenue. (What could justify such a number? The technology adoption profile, of course! For are we not just at that point in the profile where the slope is increasing at its fastest point? We don't want to lose market share at this critical juncture to some competitor. We must act while we are still within our window of opportunity. Strike while the iron is hot!) This year the company Christmas party is held at a fine hotel, the glasses are crystal, the wine vintage, and the theme, à la Dickens, is "Great Expectations."

At the beginning of the third year, a major sales force expansion is undertaken, impressive sales collateral and advertising are underwritten, district offices are opened, and customer support is strengthened. Halfway through the year, however, sales revenues are disappointing. A few more companies have come on board, but only after a prolonged sales struggle and significant compromise on price. The number of sales overall is far fewer than expected, and growth in expenses is vastly outdistancing growth in income. In the meantime, R&D is badly bogged down with several special projects committed to in the early contracts with the original customers.

Meetings are held (for the young organization is nothing if not participative in its management style). The salespeople complain that there are great holes in the product line and that what is available today is overpriced, full of bugs, and not what the customer wants. The engineers claim they have met spec and schedule for every major release, at which point the customer support staff merely groan. Executive managers lament that the sales force doesn't call high enough in the prospect organization, lacks the ability to communicate the vision, and simply isn't aggressive enough. Nothing is resolved, and, off line, political enclaves begin to form.

Third quarter revenues results are in—and they are absolutely dismal. It is time to whip the slaves. The board and the venture capitalist start in on the founders and the president, who in turn put the screws to the vice president of sales, who passes it on to the troops in the trenches. Turnover follows. The vice-president of marketing is fired. It's time to bring in "real management." More financing is required, with horrendous dilution for the initial cadre of investors—especially the founders and the key technical staff. One or more founders object but are shunted aside. Six months pass. Real management doesn't do any better. Key defections occur. Time to bring in consultants. More turnover. What we really need now, investors decide, is a turnaround artist. Layoffs followed by more turnover. And so it goes. When the screen fades to the credits, yet another venture rides off to join the twilight companies of Silicon Valley—enterprises on life support, not truly alive and yet, due in part to the vagaries of venture capital accounting, unable to choose death with dignity.

Now, it is possible that this parable overstates the case—I have been accused of such things in the past. But there is no overstating the case that year in and year out hundreds of high-tech startups, despite having good technology and exciting products, and despite initial promising returns from the market, falter and then fail. Here's why.

What the company staff interpreted as a ramp in sales leading smoothly "up the curve" was in fact an initial blip—what we will be calling the *early market*—and not the first indications of an emerging *mainstream market*. The company failed because its managers were unable to recognize that there is something fundamentally different between a sale to an early adopter and a sale to the early majority, even when the company name on the check reads the same. Thus, at a time of greatest peril, when the company was just entering the chasm, its leaders held high expectations rather than modest ones, and spent heavily in expansion projects rather than husbanding resources.

All this is the result of high-tech marketing illusion—the belief induced by the High-Tech Marketing Model that new markets unfold in a continuous and smooth way. In order to avoid the perils of the chasm, we need to achieve a new state—high-tech marketing enlightenment—by going deeper into the dynamics of the Technology Adoption Life Cycle to correct the flaws in the model and provide a secure basis for marketing strategy development.

2

High-Tech Marketing Enlightenment

> *First there is a mountain,*
> *Then there is no mountain,*
> *Then there is.*
>
> —Zen proverb

What is it about California? How can any state be so successful economically and yet so weird? I myself am from Oregon, a perfectly normal state, with a pleasantly thriving economy and plenty of fishermen and lumberjacks and such to balance out the high-tech crazies. I never intended to move south and write a book that says, in the very next paragraph mind you, that you should bet your next million on a Zen proverb. California is a bad influence.

However, if you are going to risk time and money in high tech, then you really do need to remember how high-tech markets develop, and the following proverb is as good a way as any:

First there is a market . . . Made up of innovators and early adopters, it is an early market, flush with enthusiasm and vision and, often as not, funded by a potful of dollars earmarked for accomplishing some grand strategic goal.

Then there is no market . . . This is the chasm period, during which the early market is still trying to digest its ambitious projects, and the mainstream market waits to see if anything good will come of them.

Then there is. If all goes well, and the product and your com-

27

pany pass through the chasm period intact, then a mainstream market does emerge, made up of the early and the late majority. With them comes the real opportunity for wealth and growth.

To reap the rewards of the mainstream market, your marketing strategy must successfully respond to all three of these stages. In each case, the key to success is to focus in on the dominant "adoption type" in the current phase of the market, learn to appreciate that type of person's psychographics, and then adjust your marketing strategy and tactics accordingly. Illustrating how to do that is the goal of this chapter.

First Principles

Before we get started, however, we need to establish some ground rules. The first step toward enlightenment is to get a firm grasp on the obvious. In our case, that means getting a useful working definition of the word *marketing*. *Useful* in this context means actionable—can we find in the concept of marketing a reasonable basis for taking actions that will predictably and positively affect company revenues? That, after all, is the purpose of this book.

Actually, in this context, defining marketing is not particularly difficult: It simply means taking actions to create, grow, maintain, or defend markets. What a *market* is we will get to in a moment, but it is, first, a real thing, independent of any one individual's actions. Marketing's purpose, therefore, is to develop and shape something that is real, and not, as people sometimes want to believe, to create illusions. In other words, we are dealing with a discipline more akin to gardening or sculpting than, say, to spray painting or hypnotism.

Of course, talking this way about marketing merely throws the burden of definition onto *market*, which we will define, for the purposes of high tech, as

- a set of actual or potential customers
- for a given set of products or services
- who have a common set of needs or wants, and
- who reference each other when making a buying decision.

People intuitively understand every part of this definition except the last. Unfortunately, getting the last part—the notion that part of what defines a high-tech market is the tendency of its members to reference each other when making buying decisions—is absolutely key to successful high-tech marketing. So let's make this as clear as possible.

If two people buy the same product for the same reason but have no way they could reference each other, they are not part of the same market. That is, if I sell an oscilloscope for monitoring heartbeats to a doctor in Boston and the identical product for the same purpose to a doctor in Zaire, and these two doctors have no reasonable basis for communicating with each other, then I am dealing in two different markets. Similarly, if I sell an oscilloscope to a doctor in Boston and then go next door and sell the same product to an engineer working on a sonar device, I am also dealing in two different markets. In both cases, the reason we have separate markets is because the customers could not have referenced each other.

Depending on what day of the week it is, this idea seems to be either blindingly obvious or doubtful at best. Staying with the example at hand, can't one argue that there is, after all, such a thing as the oscilloscope market? Well, yes and no. If you want to use the word *market* in this sense, it stands for the aggregate sales, both past and projected, for oscilloscopes. If that is how you want to use the word—say, if you are a financial analyst—that's fine, but you had better realize you are adding apples and oranges (that is, doctor sales + engineer sales) to get your final totals, and in so doing, you are leaving yourself open to misinterpreting the data badly. Most importantly, *market*, when it is defined in this sense, ceases to be a single, isolable object of action—it no longer refers to any single entity that can be acted on—and cannot, therefore, be the focus of *marketing*.

The way around this problem for many marketing professionals is to break up "the market" into isolable "market segments." *Market segments*, in this vocabulary, meet our definition of markets, including the self-referencing aspect. When marketing consultants sell market segmentation studies, all they are actually doing is breaking out the natural market boundaries within an aggregate of current and potential sales.

Marketing professionals insist on market segmentation because they know no meaningful marketing program can be implemented across a set of customers who do not reference each other. The reason for this is simply leverage. No company can afford to pay for every marketing contact made. Every program must rely on some ongoing chain-reaction effects—what is usually called word of mouth. The more self-referencing the market and the more tightly bounded its communications channels, the greater the opportunity for such effects.

So much for first principles. There are additional elements to our final definition of market—principally, a concept called "the whole product"—but we will get to that later in the book. For now, let's apply what we have to the three phases of high-tech marketing. The first of these is the *early market*.

Early Markets

The initial customer set for a new technology product is made up primarily of innovators and early adopters. In the high-tech industry, the innovators are better known as *technology enthusiasts* or just *techies*, whereas the early adopters are the *visionaries*. It is the latter group, the visionaries, who dominate the buying decisions in this market, but it is the technology enthusiasts who are first to realize the potential in the new product. High-tech marketing, therefore, begins with the techies.

Innovators: The Technology Enthusiasts

Classically, the first people to adopt any new technology are those who appreciate the technology for its own sake. For readers old enough to have been raised on Donald Duck comic books from Walt Disney, Gyro Gearloose may well have been your first encounter with a technology enthusiast. Or, if you were more classically educated, perhaps it was Archimedes crying, "Eureka!" at discovering the concept of measuring specific gravity through the displacement of water, or Daedalus, inventing a labyrinth and then the wings whereby one could fly out of it (if one did not fly too close to the sun). Or, for those who turn more toward movies and TV, more familiar examples of the type include *Back to the Future's* Doc Brown or the Professor from "Gilligan's Island." "Inventors," "propeller heads," "nerds," "techies"—we have many labels for a group of people who are, as a rule and despite a tendency toward introversion, delightful companions—provided you like to talk about technical topics.

They are the ones who first appreciate the architecture of your product and why it therefore has a competitive advantage over the current crop of products established in the marketplace. They are the ones who will spend hours trying to get products to work that, in all conscience, never should have been shipped in the first place. They will forgive ghastly documentation, horrendously slow performance, ludicrous omissions in functionality, and bizarrely obtuse methods of invoking some needed function—all in the name of moving technology forward. They make great critics because they truly care.

To give some high-tech examples, technology enthusiasts are the ones who buy HDTVs, DVD players, and digital cameras when they each cost well over a thousand dollars. They are interested in voice synthesis and voice recognition, interactive multimedia systems, neural networks, the modeling of chaos in Mandelbrot sets and the notion of an artificial life based on silicon. At the moment I am writing this sentence they are on the Internet at an mp3 site downloading songs to play on a Diamond R10 playback machine.

Sometimes a technology enthusiast becomes famous—usually as the inventor of a lucrative product. In the world of PCs, Bill Gates started business life this way, but he may have forfeited his status somewhat as he became more Machiavellian. Marc Andressen, on the other hand, has tried to stay more in role, although he too is looking more and more corporate. That could not be said, on the other hand, of such Internet founding stalwarts as Larry Wall the inventor of Perl, Apache cofounder Brian Behlendorf, or Linux creator Linus Torvolds. Birkenstocks forever, man, power to the people (oops, sorry, I'm having a 60s flashback).

My personal favorite, though, is a fellow named David Lichtman with whom I worked at Rand Information Systems in the late 70s and early 80s. Long before anyone was taking PCs seriously, David showed me one he had put together himself— including, as a peripheral, a voice synthesizer. This was sitting on his desk at work right next to a little microprocessor-driven box he had invented to fill out his time sheet for him. If you followed David home, you would find a house littered with cameras, sound equipment, and assorted electronic toys. And at work, whenever there was any question about how a particularly arcane or intricate tool actually functioned, David was the man to ask. He was the archetypal technology enthusiast.

In business, technology enthusiasts are the gatekeepers for any new technology. They are the ones who have the interest to learn about it and the ones everyone else deems competent to do the early evaluation. As such, they are the first key to any high-tech marketing effort.

As a buying population, or as key influences in corporate buying decisions, technology enthusiasts pose fewer requirements than any other group in the adoption profile—but you must not ignore the issues that are important to them. First, and most crucially, they want the truth, and without any tricks. Second, wherever possible, whenever they have a technical problem, they want access to the most technically knowledgeable person to answer it. Often this may not be sound from a management point of view, and you will have to deny or restrict such access, but you should never forget that it is wanted.

Third, they want to be first to get the new stuff. By working with them under nondisclosure—a commitment to which they typically adhere scrupulously—you can get great feedback early in the design cycle and begin building a supporter who will influence buyers not only in his own company but elsewhere in the marketplace as well. Finally, they want everything cheap. This is sometimes a matter of budgets, but it is more fundamentally a problem of perception—they think all technology should be free or available at cost, and they have no use for "added-value" arguments. The key consequence here is, if it is their money, you have to make it available cheap, and if it is not, you have to make sure price is not their concern.

In large companies, technology enthusiasts can most often be found in the advanced technology group, or some such congregation, chartered with keeping the company abreast of the latest developments in high tech. There they are empowered to buy one of almost anything, simply to explore its properties and examine its usefulness to the corporation. In smaller companies, which do not have such budgetary luxuries, the technology enthusiast may well be the "designated techie" in the MIS group or a member of a product design team who either will design your product in or supply it to the rest of the team as a technology aid or tool.

To reach technology enthusiasts, you need to place your message in one of their various haunts—on the Web, of course. Direct response advertising works well with this group, as they are the segment most likely to send for literature, or a free demo, or whatever you offer. Finally, don't waste your time with a lot of fancy image advertising—they read all that as just marketing hype. Direct e-mail will reach them—and provided it is factual and new information, they read cover to cover.

In sum, technology enthusiasts are easy to do business with, provided you (1) have the latest and greatest technology, and (2) don't need to make much money. For any innovation, there will always be a small class of these enthusiasts who will want to try it out *just to see if it works*. For the most part, these people are not powerful enough to dictate the buying decisions of others, nor do they represent a significant market in themselves. What they represent instead is a beachhead, a source of initial product or service references, and a test bed for introducing modifications to the product or service until it is thoroughly "debugged."

In *In Search of Excellence*, for example, Peters and Waterman tell the story of the fellow who invented Post-It notes. He just put them on the desk of secretaries, and some of those secretaries just tried them to see if or how they would work. Those secretaries became Post-It note enthusiasts and were an early key in the campaign to keep the product idea alive. Enthusiasts are like kindling: They help start the fire. They need to be cherished for that. The way to cherish them is to let them in on the secret, to let them play with the product and give you the feedback, and wherever appropriate, to implement the improvements they suggest and to let them know that you implemented them.

The other key to working with enthusiasts toward a successful marketing campaign is to find the ones who are near or have access to *the big boss*. Big bosses are people who can dictate purchases and who do represent a significant marketing opportunity in and of themselves. To get more specific about the kind of big boss we are looking for, let us now turn to the next group in the Technology Adoption Life Cycle, the *early adopters*, or as they are often called in the high-tech industry, the *visionaries*.

Early Adopters: The Visionaries

Visionaries are that rare breed of people who have the insight to match an emerging technology to a strategic opportunity, the temperament to translate that insight into a high-visibility, high-risk project, and the charisma to get the rest of their organization to buy into that project. They are the early adopters of high-tech products. Often working with budgets in the multiple millions of dollars, they represent a hidden source of venture capital that funds high-technology business.

When John F. Kennedy launched the U.S. space program, he showed himself to be something we in America had not known for some time—a visionary president. When Henry T. Ford implemented factory-line mass production of automobiles so that every family in America could afford one, he became one of our best-known business visionaries. When Steve Jobs took the Xerox PARC interface out of the laboratory and put it into a personal computer "for the rest of us," then drove the rest of the PC industry to accept this computer almost in spite of itself, he showed himself to be a visionary to be reckoned with.

As a class, visionaries tend to be recent entrants to the executive ranks, highly motivated, and driven by a "dream." The core of the dream is a business goal, not a technology goal, and it involves taking a quantum leap forward in how business is conducted in their industry or by their customers. It also involves a high degree of personal recognition and reward. Understand their dream, and you will understand how to market to them.

To give additional examples specific to high tech, when Sheldon Laube at Price Waterhouse committed to purchase and install ten thousand copies of Lotus's new and totally unproven product, Notes, he was acting as a visionary. When Pete Solvik, CIO at Cisco, drove all the customer service and order processing systems to the Internet, abandoning client-server computing even before it had reached its peak, he was acting as a visionary. When Jim Barksdale at Federal Express opened up their customer service systems to self-service, first via a PC then via the Web, he was acting as a visionary. In every case, these people took significant business risks with what at the time was unproven technology in order to achieve breakthrough improvements in productivity and customer service.

And that is the key point. Visionaries are not looking for an *improvement;* they are looking for a fundamental *breakthrough.* Technology is important only insomuch as it promises to deliver on this dream. If the dream is cell phone usage anywhere, then the system will involve a matrix of Low-Earth-Orbit satellites such as Iridium or Teledesic. If it is one-on-one marketing, then the technology will include data mining of transaction-processing databases such as that provided by BM's Intelligent Miner. If it is an inventoryless supply chain then it will include advanced planning, forecasting, and replenishment algorithms combined to intercompany systems integration as companies like Manugistics and I2 bring to market. If it is eliminating the paperwork nightmare of agent-based insurance sales, then it will include self-service technology from the Internet and legacy systems integration such as Channelpoint is introducing. The key point is that, in contrast with the technology enthusiast, a visionary derives value not from a system's technology itself but from the strategic leap forward it enables.

Visionaries drive the high-tech industry because they see the potential for an "order-of-magnitude" return on investment and willingly take high risks to pursue that goal. They will work with vendors who have little or no funding, with products that start life as little more than a diagram on a whiteboard, and with technology gurus who bear a disconcerting resemblance to Rasputin. They know they are going outside the mainstream, and they accept that as part of the price you pay when trying to leapfrog the competition.

Because they see such vast potential for the technology they have in mind, they are the least price-sensitive of any segment of the technology adoption profile. They typically have budgets that let them allocate generous amounts toward the implementation of a strategic initiative. This means they can usually provide upfront money to seed additional development that supports their project—hence their importance as a source of high-tech development capital.

Finally, beyond fueling the industry with dollars, visionaries are also effective at alerting the business community to pertinent technology advances. Outgoing and ambitious as a group, they are usually more than willing to serve as highly visible references, thereby drawing the attention of the business press and additional customers to small fledgling enterprises.

As a buying group, visionaries are easy to sell but very hard to please. This is because they are buying a dream—which, to some degree, will always be a dream. The "incarnation" of this dream will require the melding of numerous technologies, many of which will be immature or even nonexistent at the beginning of the project. The odds against everything falling into place without a hitch are astronomical. Nonetheless, both the buyer and the seller can build successfully on two key principles.

First, visionaries like a project orientation. They want to start out with a pilot project, which makes sense because they are "going where no man has gone before" and you are going with them. This is followed by more project work, conducted in phases, with milestones, and the like. The visionaries' idea is to be able to stay very close to the development train to make sure it is going in the right direction and to be able to get off if they discover it is not going where they thought.

While reasonable from the customer's point of view, this project orientation is usually at odds with the entrepreneurial vendors who are trying to create a more universally applicable product around which they can build a multicustomer business. This potentially lose/lose situation—threatening both the quality of the vendor's work and the fabric of the relationship—requires careful account management, including frequent contact at the executive level.

The winning strategy is built around the entrepreneur being able to "productize" the deliverables from each phase of the visionary project. That is, whereas for the visionary the deliverables of phase one are only of marginal interest—proof of concept with some productivity improvement gained, but not "the vision"— these same deliverables, repackaged, can be a whole product to someone with less ambitious goals. For example, a company might be developing a comprehensive object-oriented software toolkit, capable of building systems that could model the entire workings of a manufacturing plant, thereby creating an order-of-magnitude improvement in scheduling and processing efficiency. The first deliverable of the toolkit might be a model of just one milling machine's operations and its environment. The visionary looks at that model as a milestone. But the vendor of that milling machine might look at the same model as a very desirable product alterations and want to license it with only modest alterations. It is important, therefore, in creating the phases of the visionary's project to build in milestones that lend themselves to this sort of product spin-off.

The other key quality of visionaries is that they are in a hurry. They see the future in terms of windows of opportunity, and they see those windows closing. As a result, they tend to exert deadline pressures—the carrot of a big payment or the stick of a penalty clause—to drive the project faster. This plays into the classic weaknesses of entrepreneurs—lust after the big score and overconfidence in their ability to execute within any given time frame.

Here again, account management and executive restraint are crucial. The goal should be to package each of the phases such that each phase

1. is accomplishable by mere mortals working in earth time
2. provides the vendor with a marketable product
3. provides the customer with a concrete return on investment that can be celebrated as a major step forward.

The last point is crucial. Getting closure with visionaries is next to impossible. Expectations derived from dreams simply cannot be met. This is not to devalue the dream, for without it there would be no directing force to drive progress of any sort. What is important is to celebrate continually the tangible and partial as both useful things in their own right and as heralds of the new order to come.

The most important principle stemming from all this is the emphasis on management of expectations. Because controlling expectations is so crucial, the only practical way to do business with visionaries is through a small, top-level direct sales force. At the front end of the sales cycle, you need such a group to understand the visionaries' goals and give them confidence that your company can step up to them. In the middle of the sales cycle, you need to be extremely flexible about commitments as you begin to adapt to the visionaries' agenda. At the end, you need to be very careful in negotiations, keeping the spark of the vision alive without committing to tasks that are unachievable within the time frame allotted. All this implies a mature and sophisticated representative working on your behalf.

In terms of prospecting for visionaries, they are not likely to have a particular job title, except that, to be truly useful, they must have achieved at least a vice presidential level in order to have the clout to fund their visions. In fact, in terms of communications, typically you don't find them, they find you. The way they find you, interestingly enough, is by maintaining relationships with technology enthusiasts. That is one of the reasons why it is so important to capture the technology enthusiast segment.

In sum, visionaries represent an opportunity early in a product's life cycle to generate a burst of revenue and gain exceptional visibility. The opportunity comes with a price tag—a highly demanding customer who will seek to influence your company's priorities directly and a high-risk project that could end in disappointment for all. But without this boost many high-tech products cannot make it to market, unable to gain the visibility they need within their window of opportunity, or unable to sustain their financial obligations while waiting for their marketplace to develop more slowly. Visionaries are the ones who give high-tech companies their first big break. It is hard to plan for them in marketing programs, but it is even harder to plan without them.

The Dynamics of Early Markets

To get an early market started requires an entrepreneurial company with a breakthrough technology product that enables a new and compelling application, a technology enthusiast who can evaluate and appreciate the superiority of the product over current alternatives, and a well-heeled visionary who can foresee an order-of-magnitude improvement from implementing the new application. When the market is unfolding as it should, the entrepreneurial company seeds the technology enthusiast community with early copies of its product while at the same time sharing its vision with the visionary executives. It then invites the visionary executives to check with the technology enthusiast of their choice to verify that the vision is indeed achievable. Out of these conversations comes a series of negotiations in which, for what seems like a very large amount of money at the time, but which will later be recognized as just the tip of the iceberg, the technology enthusiasts get to buy more toys than they have ever dreamed of, the entrepreneurial company commits itself to product modifications and system integration services it never intended to, and the visionary has what on paper looks to be an achievable project, but which is in fact a highly improbable dream.

That's when the market unfolds as it should. That is the good scenario—good because, although it is rife with problems, they are ones that will get solved one way or another, and some level of value will be achieved all around. There are numerous other scenarios where the early market does not even get a proper start. Here are some of them:

- First problem: The company simply has no expertise in bringing a product to market. It raises insufficient capital for the effort, hires inexperienced sales and marketing people, tries to sell the product through an inappropriate channel of distribution, promotes in the wrong places and in the wrong ways, and in general fouls things up.

  Remedying this kind of situation is not as hard as it may seem, provided the participants in the company are still communicating and cooperating with each other, and everyone is willing to scale back their expectations several notches.

  The basis for reform is the principle that winning at marketing more often than not means being the biggest fish in the pond. If we are very small, then we must search out a very small pond indeed. To qualify as a "real pond," as we also noted before, its members must be aware of themselves as a group, that is, it must constitute a self-referencing market segment, so that when we establish a leadership position with some of its members, they will get the word out—quickly and economically—to the rest.

  Of course, no single pond of a size we can dominate in the short term is large enough to provide a sustaining market for the long term. Sooner or later, we have to go "pond hopping." Or, to shift the metaphor, we need to reframe our "pond" tactics in the context of a "bowling pin" strategy, where one targets a given segment not just because one can "knock it over" but because, in so doing, it will help knock over the next target segment, and thus lead to market expansion. With the right kind of angle of attack, it is amazing how large and fast the chain reaction can be. So one is never necessarily out of the game, even when things are pretty bleak.

- A second problem: The company sells the visionary before it has the product. This is a version of the famous *vaporware* problem, based on preannouncing and premarketing a product that still has significant development hurdles to overcome. At best, the entrepreneurial company secures a few pilot projects, but as schedules continue to slip, the visionary's position in the organization weakens, and support for the project is eventually withdrawn, despite a lot of customized work, with no usable customer reference gained.

Caught in this situation, the entrepreneurial company has only one adequate response, a truly unhappy one: shut down its marketing efforts, admit its mistakes to its investors, and focus all its energies into turning its pilot projects into something useful, first in terms of a deliverable to the customer, and ultimately in terms of a marketable product. Since most entrepreneurial companies are fueled, as much as anything, on the ego of their founders, this is too often the road not taken, thereby keeping bankruptcy lawyers—and, sadder still, frequently divorce lawyers—in full employment.

• Problem number three: Marketing falls prey to the crack between the technology enthusiast and the visionary by failing to discover, or at least failing to articulate, the compelling application that provides the order-of-magnitude leap in benefits. A number of companies buy the product to test it out, but it never gets incorporated into a major system rollout, because the rewards never quite measure up to the risks. The resulting lack of revenue leads to folding the effort, either by shutting it down entirely, or selling it off "for scrap" to another enterprise.

The corrective response here begins with reevaluating what we have. If it is not, in fact, a breakthrough product, then it is not ever going to create an early market. But perhaps it could serve as a supplementary product in an existing mainstream market. If that is indeed the case, then the right response is to swallow our pride, reduce our financial expectations, and subordinate ourselves to an existing mainstream-market company, who can put our product in play through its existing channels. Computer Associates, one of the largest software companies in the world, was built up almost entirely on this principle of remarketing other companies' often cast-off products.

Alternatively, if we truly have a breakthrough product, but we are stalled in getting the early market moving, then we have to step down from the lofty theoretical plateau on which we have established that this product can be part of any number of exciting applications. Then we must get very practical about focusing on one application, making sure that it is indeed a compelling one for at least one visionary who is already familiar with us, and then committing to that visionary, in return for his or her support, to removing every obstacle to getting that application adopted.

These are some of the most common ways in which an early market development effort can go off—and be put back on—track. For the most part, the problems are solvable because there are always multiple options at the outset of anything. The biggest problem is typically overly ambitious expectations combined with undercapitalization—or, as my grandmother used to put it, when your eyes are bigger than your stomach. Things get a lot more complex when we are dealing with the dynamics of mainstream markets, to which we shall now turn.

Mainstream Markets

Mainstream markets in high tech look a lot like mainstream markets in any other industry, particularly those that sell business to business. They are dominated by the early majority, who in high tech are best understood as *pragmatists*, who, in turn, tend to be accepted as leaders by the late majority, best thought of as *conservatives*, and rejected as leaders by the laggards, or *skeptics*. As in the previous chapter, we are going to look closely at how the psychographics of each of these groups influences the development and dynamics of a high-tech market.

Early Majority: The Pragmatists

Throughout the 1980s, the early majority, or pragmatists, have represented the bulk of the market volume for any technology product. You can succeed with the visionaries, and you can thereby get a reputation for being a high flyer with a hot product, but that is not ultimately where the dollars are. Instead, those funds are in the hands of more prudent souls, who do not want to be pioneers ("Pioneers are people with arrows in their backs"), who never volunteer to be an early test site ("Let somebody else debug your product"), and who have learned the hard way that the "leading edge" of technology is all too often the "bleeding edge."

Who are the pragmatists? Actually, important as they are, they are hard to characterize because they do not have the visionary's penchant for drawing attention to themselves. They are not the Hamlets but the Horatios, not the Don Quixotes but the Sancho Panzas, a character more like the *X-File*'s Dana Scully than Fox Mulder, more like *Lethal Weapon*'s Sergeant Murtaugh than Martin Riggs—people who do not assert a position in life so much as derive one from what life provides. Never the standout, they are what makes for the continuity, so that after the star either dies (tragedy) or rides off into the sunset (heroic romance, comedy), they are left to clean up and to answer the inevitable final question: Who was that masked man?

In the realm of high tech, pragmatist CEOs are not common, and those there are, true to their type, tend to keep a relatively low profile. Ray Lane of Oracle (as opposed to Larry Ellison), Craig Barrett of Intel (as opposed to Andy Grove), Lew Platt of Hewlett-Packard (as opposed to Scott McNealy at Sun), and Carol Bartz on Autodesk all come to mind. They tend to be best known by their closest colleagues, from whom they typically have earned the highest respect, and by their peers within their industry, where they show up near the top of the leader board year after year.

Of course, to market successfully to pragmatists, one does not have to be one—just understand their values and work to serve them. To look more closely into these values, if the goal of visionaries is to take a quantum leap forward, the goal of pragmatists is to make a percentage improvement—incremental, measurable, predictable progress. If they are installing a new product, they want to know how other people have fared with it. The word *risk* is a negative word in their vocabulary—it does not connote opportunity or excitement but rather the chance to waste money and time. They will undertake risks when required, but they first will put in place safety nets and manage the risks very closely.

The Fortune 2000 MIS community, as a group, is led by people who are largely pragmatist in orientation. Business demands for increased productivity push them toward the front of the adoption life cycle, but natural prudence and budget restrictions keep them cautious. As individuals, pragmatists held back from buying Windows until Release 3.0, held back from client/server applications until PeopleSoft, Oracle, and SAP gave three safe choices, and are still trying to figure out today how far to let the Internet into their corporate environments.

If pragmatists are hard to win over, they are loyal once won, often enforcing a company standard that requires the purchase of your product, and only your product, for a given requirement. This focus on standardization is, well, pragmatic, in that it simplifies internal service demands. But the secondary effects of this standardization—increasing sales volumes and lowering the cost of sales—is dramatic. Hence the importance of pragmatists as a market segment.

The most celebrated example and beneficiary of this effect in the last decade has been Microsoft. We tend to think of Microsoft's dominance in operating systems as exclusive today, but actually, as the desktop and workgroup server markets were developing, they supported a variety of vendors, each with its own pragmatist enclave. In the engineering community, they gravitated to Sun's Solaris; in the graphics community, to Apple's Macintosh OS; in the workgroup, to Novell Netware; in the Fortune 500 replicated-site environments of branch banking and retail, to OS/2; in the VAR-dominated professional services systems for doctors and dentists, to SCO Unix. Each one of these companies rode a pragmatist wave within a specific market to boost its sales a quantum leap upward. It is crucial, therefore, for any long-term strategic marketing plan to understand the pragmatist buyers and to focus on winning their trust.

When pragmatists buy, they care about the company they are buying from, the quality of the product they are buying, the infrastructure of supporting products and system interfaces, and the reliability of the service they are going to get. In other words, they are planning on living with this decision personally for a long time to come. (By contrast, the visionaries are more likely to be planning on implementing the great new order and then using that as a springboard to their next great career step upward.) Because pragmatists are in it for the long haul, and because they control the bulk of the dollars in the marketplace, the rewards for building relationships of trust with them are very much worth the effort.

Pragmatists tend to be "vertically" oriented, meaning that they communicate more with others like themselves within their own industry than do technology enthusiasts and early adopters, who are more likely to communicate "horizontally" across industry boundaries in search of kindred spirits. This means it is very tough to break into a new industry selling to pragmatists. References and relationships are very important to these people, and there is a kind of catch-22 operating: Pragmatists won't buy from you until you are established, yet you can't get established until they buy from you. Obviously, this works to the disadvantage of start-ups and, conversely, to the great advantage of companies with established track records. On the other hand, once a start-up has earned its spurs with the pragmatist buyers within a given vertical market, they tend to be very loyal to it, and even go out of their way to help it succeed. When this happens, the cost of sales goes way down, and the leverage on incremental R&D to support any given customer goes way up. That's one of the reasons pragmatists make such a great market.

There is no one distribution channel preferred by pragmatists, but they do want to keep the sum total of their distribution relationships to a minimum. This allows them to maximize their buying leverage and maintain a few clear points of control, should anything go wrong. In some cases this prejudice can be overcome if the pragmatist buyer knows a particular salesperson from a previous relationship. As a rule, however, the path into the pragmatist community is smoother if a smaller entrepreneurial vendor can develop an alliance with one of the already accepted vendors or if it can establish a value-added-reseller (VAR) sales base. VARs, if they truly specialize in the pragmatist's particular industry, and if they have a reputation for delivering quality work on time and within budget, represent an extremely attractive type of solution to a pragmatist. They can provide a "turnkey" answer to a problem, without impacting internal resources already overloaded with the burdens of ongoing system maintenance. What the pragmatist likes best about VARs is that they represent a single point of control, a single company to call if anything goes wrong.

One final characteristic of pragmatist buyers is that they like to see competition—in part to get costs down, in part to have the security of more than one alternative to fall back on, should anything go wrong, and in part to assure themselves they are buying from a proven market leader. This last point is crucial: Pragmatists want to buy from proven market leaders because they know that third parties will design supporting products around a market-leading product. That is, market-leading products create an *aftermarket* that other vendors service. This radically reduces pragmatist customers' burden of support. By contrast, if they mistakenly choose a product that does not become the market leader, but rather one of the also-rans, then this highly valued aftermarket support does not develop, and they will be stuck making all the enhancements by themselves. Market leadership is crucial, therefore, to winning pragmatist customers.

Pragmatists are reasonably price-sensitive. They are willing to pay a modest premium for top quality or special services, but in the absence of any special differentiation, they want the best deal. That's because, having typically made a career commitment to their job and/or their company, they get measured year in and year out on what their operation has spent versus what it has returned to the corporation.

Overall, to market to pragmatists, you must be patient. You need to be conversant with the issues that dominate their particular business. You need to show up at the industry-specific conferences and trade shows they attend. You need to be mentioned in articles that run in the magazines they read. You need to be installed in other companies in their industry. You need to have developed applications for your product that are specific to the industry. You need to have partnerships and alliances with the other vendors who serve their industry. You need to have earned a reputation for quality and service. In short, you need to make yourself over into the obvious supplier of choice.

This is a long-term agenda, requiring careful pacing, recurrent investment, and a mature management team. One of its biggest payoffs, on the other hand, is that it not only delivers the pragmatist element of the Technology Adoption Life Cycle but tees up the conservative element as well. Sadly, however, high-tech industry has, for the most part, not seen fit to reap the rewards it has so carefully sown. To see how this has come about, let us now take a closer look at the conservatives.

Late Majority: The Conservatives

The mathematics of the Technology Adoption Life Cycle model says that for every pragmatist there is a conservative. Put another way, conservatives represent approximately one-third of the total available customers within any given Technology Adoption Life Cycle. As a marketable segment, however, they are rarely developed as profitably as they could be, largely because high-tech companies are not, as a rule, in sympathy with them.

Conservatives, in essence, are against discontinuous innovations. They believe far more in tradition than in progress. And when they find something that works for them, they like to stick with it. Most people in high tech think of Esther Dyson, for example, as a visionary, but when it comes to word processing, she is a conservative—clinging to using Xywrite, her original word processor from the early 1980s, long after the rest of us were on Microsoft Word. It works for her, and that is the key criterion. I personally feel the same way about America Online. Among the technochic, AOL is very unchic, but it works for me.

In this sense, conservatives have more in common with early adopters than one might think. Both can be stubborn in their resistance to the call to conform that unites the pragmatist herd. To be sure, in many cases both do succumb to the new paradigm, long after it was really new, just to stay on par with the rest of the world. But just because conservatives use such products, they don't necessarily have to like them.

The truth is, conservatives often fear high tech a little bit. Therefore, they tend to invest only at the end of a technology life cycle, when products are extremely mature, market-share competition is driving low prices, and the products themselves can be treated as commodities. Often their real goal in buying high-tech products is simply not to get stung. Unfortunately, because they are working the low-margin end of the market, where there is little motive for the seller to build a high-integrity relationship with the buyer, they often do get stung. This only reinforces their disillusion with high tech and resets the buying cycle at an even more cynical level.

If high-tech businesses are going to be successful over the long term, they must learn to break this vicious circle and establish a reasonable basis for conservatives to want to do business with them. They must understand that conservatives do not have high aspirations about their high-tech investments and hence will not support high price margins. Nonetheless, through sheer volume, they can offer great rewards to the companies that serve them appropriately.

It is easy to understand conservatives if you can observe some aspect of their buying behavior within yourself. In my case, I am a late adopter of many kinds of consumer products. I did not buy my first CD until 1998. I carry a pager but do not give out the number. I carry a cell phone but never turn it on. When offered a GPS navigational option on my car, I declined. In general, I hate "being connected," which I associate with being either interrupted or confused, not being in touch. And thus there are whole chunks of consumer technology that I want no part of. I'm uncomfortable with most types of personal finance transactions, and I'm a very late adopter of any new kind of investment opportunity. Getting in touch with feelings like these helps one market to conservatives.

Conservatives like to buy preassembled packages, with everything bundled, at a heavily discounted price. The last thing they want to hear is that the software they just bought doesn't support the printer they have installed. They want high-tech products to be like refrigerators—you open the door, the light comes on automatically, your food stays cold, and you don't have to think about it. The products they understand best are those dedicated to a single function—word processors, calculators, copiers, and fax machines. The notion that a single computer could do all four of these functions does not excite them—instead, it is something they find vaguely nauseating.

The conservative marketplace provides a great opportunity, in this regard, to take low-cost, trailing-edge technology components and repackage them into single-function systems for specific business needs. The quality of the package should be quite high because there is nothing in it that has not already been thoroughly debugged. The price should be quite low because all the R&D has long since been amortized, and every bit of the manufacturing learning curve has been taken advantage of. It is, in short, not just a pure marketing ploy but a true solution for a new class of customer.

There are two keys to success here. The first is to have thoroughly thought through the "whole solution" to a particular target end user market's needs, and to have provided for every element of that solution within the package. This is critical because there is no profit margin to support an afterpurchase support system. The other key is to have lined up a low-overhead distribution channel that can get this package to the target market effectively.

Conservatives have enormous value to high-tech industry in that they greatly extend the market for high-tech components that are no longer state-of-the-art. The fact that the United States has all but conceded great hunks of this market to the Far East is testimony not so much to the cost advantages of offshore manufacturing as to the failure of onshore product planning and marketing imagination. Many Far East solutions today still bring only one value to the table—low cost. That is, they are nowhere near the goal of being a "whole product solution." Thus, they typically have to go through a VAR channel in order to be upgraded to the kind of complete system that a conservative can purchase. The difficulty in this distribution strategy is that few VARs are large enough to achieve the volume needed to leverage a conservative market. Far more dollars could be mined from this segment of the high-tech marketplace if American leading-edge manufacturers and marketers, with their high-volume channels and vast purchasing resources, simply paid more attention to it.

So, the conservative market is still something that high-tech has in its future more than in its past. To be sure, a few companies have staked out their claims. Xerox and the rest of the copier industry, despite their outward emphasis on "going digital," still use strong distribution channel services to stay close to conservative customers, offering to outsource the operations of anything that seems too daunting to handle in house. Cell phones have now reached sufficient saturation of the pragmatist market to reach out to conservatives with popular offers such as a AAA phone which has a dedicated button for calling for roadside service, an offer that cuts through the conservatives technoanxiety to allay another set of fears. And purveyors to the home PC market have come a long way in orchestrating the "out of box" experience such that a non-technical person can get up and running—and have a successful first experience—within 20 minutes. Witness our recent purchase of an iMac where the toughest decision was choosing the color (grape).

Despite such successes, however, one has the feeling that the conservative market is perceived more as a burden than an opportunity. High-tech business success within it will require a new kind of marketing imagination linked to a less venturesome financial model. The dollars are there for the making if we can meet new challenges that are as yet only partially familiar. However, as the cost of R&D radically escalates, companies are going to have to amortize that cost across bigger and bigger markets, and this must inevitably lead to the long ignored "back half" of the technology adoption curve.

The Dynamics of Mainstream Markets

Just as the visionaries drive the development of the early market, so do the pragmatists drive the development of the mainstream market. Winning their support is not only the point of entry but the key to long-term dominance. But having done so, you cannot take the market for granted.

To maintain leadership in a mainstream market, you must at least keep pace with the competition. It is no longer necessary to be the technology leader, nor is it necessary to have the very best product. But the product must be *good enough*, and should a competitor make a major breakthrough, you have to make at least a catch-up response.

No one is better at playing this game than Oracle Corporation and its president, Larry Ellison. Oracle won the pragmatist market away from Relational Technology Inc. (now called ASK Ingres) by virtue of a single brilliant move—standardizing on SQL as its interface language. Because IBM was driving SQL to become a standard, Oracle could ride their coattails. But then it went one step further. It ported Oracle—and the SQL interface—to every piece of hardware it could find, something IBM could not, or at least certainly would not, consider doing. This appeared to solve what was rapidly becoming the single biggest headache for pragmatists—the proliferation of incompatible systems that, sooner or later, would have to be made to communicate with each other. Everyone and his mother wanted to be the glue to hold these systems together; Oracle won the job.

Having done so, however, Oracle did not sit back and take the market for granted. The independent software vendors at Ingres, Informix, and Sybase, not to mention the in-house database groups at IBM, DEC, Tandem, and Hewlett-Packard, were coming after them. Ingres came out with Ingres/Net and Ingres/Star to provide the data communications gateways to link the incompatible systems. Oracle responded with SQL*Star and SQL*Net. Did they actually have comparable products? No, but neither really did Ingres—they had preannounced. By the time real product started getting to real customers, Oracle was already on the way to closing the technology gap. Besides, most pragmatists did not want to undertake all this linking right away—they just wanted to know there was a growth path in the works. As long as Oracle could demonstrate that, they could keep the leadership position.

Along came Sybase and took a technology leadership position in something called distributed on-line transaction processing based on client/server architecture. Never mind that at present this is a relatively small niche market: It is technologically where the future of database systems is headed. Once again, Oracle did not ignore this potential threat. It announced its own client/server architecture—indeed, claimed it had had it all along—and again, just the *plan* for such a topology has been enough to keep the mainstream market reasonably well under control.

Of course, Oracle did not invent this sort of strategy. The credit there, at least for high tech, has to go to its greatest practitioner, IBM.

Nevertheless, few companies have been as competitive as Oracle. Indeed, several have shown how you can lose a mainstream market, despite everyone's efforts, including your own customers', to prevent that. Here are some of the more common ways:

- *Stop investing in the market, cease funding R&D to match the competition, and milk it for money to invest elsewhere.* This is what Novell did with its core Netware business in the Local Area Network market. Once it had established market leadership there, it shifted its focus to porting to mainframe and minicomputers, to buying up other applications (notably WordPerfect) and other operating systems (Unix), and to futuristic dreams like NEST for home appliance networking. All the while Microsoft NT was looming as a workgroup alternative. The key to defending this market was for Novell to improve Netware's support for database applications, a technology called Netware Loadable Modules, that for years had limped along and really needed refurbishing. But Novell never found time for that, whereas Microsoft, by linking its SQL Server to its NT offer, did. When NT finally began to displace the Netware server, Novell woke up, but by then it was too late. As the century comes to a close, the company is trying to rebuild a franchise around some superb offerings in directory services, but it is working from a position of weakness for which it has only itself to blame.

- *Shoot yourself in the flagship product.* This is what Autodesk did with Release 13 of AutoCad, the industry standard for PC-based mechanical and industrial design. The company had lagged technology development in prior releases and targeted this one to make up for lost ground by introducing 3D CAD along with a host of other changes and additions. The product was confusing, its performance was embarrassingly slow, the customers stayed away in droves, and Autodesk's distribution partners hit the roof.

But here is where a commitment to market leadership pays off. Despite all the criticism Autodesk got, nobody defected from their camp. They just beat them up and withheld their dollars. And so the company hunkered down, got an interim performance release out, and then launched Release 14, which got gold stars. Since that release it has been enjoying a surge in sales (essentially recouping much of what it had previously left on the table), and is back on track.

The key point here is that mainstream customers truly abhor discontinuous innovations. Switching to another PC CAD system will be incredibly disruptive to their operations, whether they are an in-house operation or a VAP of systems that incorporate AutoCad. By righting its ship and staying its course Autodesk was able to leverage these switching costs to its advantage and reassert its market position.

Novell and Autodesk both made serious marketing errors that jeopardized their mainstream-market leadership positions. Why? Part of the answer has to be that they were thinking with the wrong marketing model. Their decisions showed them to be overly focused on what was going on in early markets and too inattentive to the underdeveloped elements in the mainstream. In particular, they were not paying any attention at all to extending their market share to incorporate more conservatives.

There has been some improvement in mainstream marketing to conservatives during this last decade, but it is still more the exception than the rule. To be fair, in many parts of high tech technology adoption life cycles come rolling in one after another so fast that it seems there is no time for Main Street. But that is more perception than reality. Take the case of the proprietary minicomputer. Surely, with the advent of Unix and NT, these products should be dead as doornails. And indeed, some very fine ones are—Wang, Prime, Apollo, Convex, Data General, and even Digital are all basically on the shelf. But in the midst of this, as the century comes to a close, two franchises—the AS/400 and the HP 3000—are *resurging!* Both have made concerted efforts to market directly to conservatives. They have both taken technology developed by other divisions (thereby keeping their incremental costs low) to keep their platforms up to current performance standards. At the same time, they have leveraged their installed base of applications to nurture loyal customers and even get some new ones. Customer service is key to their business, as is the ability to make add-on offers that incrementally upgrade capabilities without technological risk—more disk space, more memory, links to client-server systems, links to the Internet—all outboard of the core system which lies relatively untouched, chugging along, reliable as all get out, and fully paid for.

The key to making a smooth transition from the pragmatist to the conservative market segments is to maintain a strong relationship with the former, always giving them an open door to go to the new paradigm, while still keeping the latter happy by adding value to the old infrastructure. It is a balancing act to say the least, but properly managed the earnings potential in loyal mature market segments is very high indeed.

In this regard, if we now look back over the first four profiles in the Technology Adoption Life Cycle, we see an interesting trend. The importance of the product itself, its unique functionality, when compared to the importance of the ancillary services to the customer, is at its highest with the technology enthusiast, and, at its lowest with the conservative. This is no surprise, since one's level of involvement and competence with a high-tech product are a prime indicator of when one will enter the Technology Adoption Life Cycle. The key lesson is that the longer your product is in the market, the more mature it becomes, and the more important the service element is to the customer. Conservatives, in particular, are extremely service oriented.

Now, it would be a much simpler world if conservatives were willing to pay for all this service they require. But they are not. So the corollary lesson is, we must use our experience with the pragmatist customer segment to identify all the issues that require service and then design solutions to these problems directly into the product. This must be the focus of mature market R&D—not the extension of functionality, not the massive rewrite from the ground up, but the gradual incorporation into the product of all the little aids that people develop, often on their own, to help them cope with its limitations. This is service indeed, for the best service, both from the point of view of convenience to the customer and low cost to the vendor, is no service at all.

Not following this path makes us vulnerable to the crack in the bell curve that separates pragmatists from conservatives. The latter are not anxious to admit to their pragmatist friends that they are unwilling or unable to step up to the same level of technological self-support, but that is in fact one of the key differentiating factors between the two groups. To date, high tech has not widely acknowledged this gap, with the result that the industry has experienced product life cycles that are far shorter than need be, and revenue streams that are far more dependent on the success of new products, and hence far more volatile, than in other industries.

All that being said, it is to high tech's inability to transition its marketing efforts effectively between the pragmatists and the conservatives that poses the greatest threat to its well-being. That honor, as we shall see in the next chapter, goes to another transition in the Technology Adoption Life Cycle, the place where high-tech fortunes truly are made or lost, crossing the chasm between the early market with its visionaries and the mainstream market with its pragmatists. Before passing on, however, to our main theme, there is one last element in the Technology Adoption Life Cycle that deserves at least a passing comment.

Laggards: The Skeptics

Skeptics—the group that makes up the last one-sixth of the Technology Adoption Life Cycle—do not participate in the high-tech marketplace, except to block purchases. Thus, the primary function of high-tech marketing in relation to skeptics is to neutralize their influence. In a sense, this is a pity because skeptics can teach us a lot about what we are doing wrong—hence this postscript.

One of the favorite arguments of skeptics is that the billions of dollars invested in office automation have not improved the productivity of the office place one iota. Actually, some fairly good data exist to support this notion. Nonetheless, as you might expect, this argument outrages high-tech supporters, who can point to any number of obvious ways in which the industry eliminates or facilitates routine—or even nonroutine—office chores. But what if, instead of rushing to rebuttal, marketing were to explore the merits of the skeptic's argument?

What we might find, for example, is that while high-tech products do give time back to the individual, the individual does not necessarily give that time back to the corporation. Or we might find that the capabilities designed and manufactured into the system at great expense remain buried in the system because the user never learns about them. Or we might find that for every individual who can transform the hours invested in training into competence in a high-tech product, there might be another who cannot. The loss associated with these people is high, considering not just their time spent in training, along with any trainer time, but also the cost of the system bought to support them, the system they cannot effectively use.

The point is, as any experienced seller of high-tech products can tell you, cost-justification of high-tech purchases is a shaky venture at best. There is always the potential to return significant dollars, but it always depends on factors beyond the system itself. Put another way, this simply means that the claims that salespeople made for high-tech products are really claims made for "whole product solutions" that incorporate elements well beyond whatever high-tech manufacturers ship inside their boxes. If high-tech marketers do not take responsibility for seeing that the whole product solution is being delivered, then they are giving the skeptic an opening to block the sale. (For all the reasons just cited the significance of whole product solutions is discussed at length later as the key component of successfully crossing the chasm and entering into the mainstream.)

What skeptics are struggling to point out is that new systems, for the most part, don't deliver on the promises that were made at the time of their purchase. This is not to say they do not end up delivering value, but rather that the value they actually deliver is not often anticipated at the time of purchase. If this is true— and to some degree I believe it is—it means that committing to a new system is a much greater act of faith than normally imagined. It means that the primary value in the act derives more from such notions as supporting a bias toward action than from any quantifiable packet of cost-justified benefits. The idea that the value of the system will be discovered rather than known at the time of installation implies, in turn, that product flexibility and adaptability, as well as ongoing account service, should be critical components of any buyer's evaluation checklist.

Ultimately the service that skeptics provide to high-tech marketers is to point continually to the discrepancies between the sales claims and the delivered product. These discrepancies, in turn, create opportunities for the customer to fail, and such failures, through word of mouth, will ultimately come back to haunt us as lost market share. Steamrolling over the skeptics, in other words, may be a great sales tactic, but it is a poor marketing one. From a marketing point of view, we are all subject to the "Emperor's New Clothes" syndrome, but particularly so in high tech, where every player in the market has a vested interest in boosting the overall perception of the industry. Skeptics don't buy our act. We ought to take advantage of that fact.

Back to the Chasm

As the preceding pages indicate, there is clearly a lot of value in the Technology Adoption Life Cycle as a marketing model. By isolating the psychographics of customers based on when they tend to enter the market, it gives clear guidance on how to develop a marketing program for an innovative product.

The basic flaw in the model, as we have said, is that it implies a smooth and continuous progression across segments over the life of a product, whereas experience teaches just the opposite. Indeed, making the marketing and communications transition between any two adoption segments is normally excruciatingly awkward because you must adopt new strategies just at the time you have become most comfortable with the old ones.

The biggest problem during this transition period is the lack of a customer base that can be referenced at the time of making the transition into a new segment. As we saw when we redrew the Technology Adoption Life Cycle, the spaces between segments indicate the credibility gap that arises from seeking to use the group on the left as a reference base to penetrate the segment on the right.

In some cases, the basic affinities of the market keep groups relatively close together. Early adopting visionaries, for example, tend to keep in touch with and respect the views of technology enthusiasts; this is because they need the latter to serve as a reality check on the technical feasibility of their vision and to help evaluate specific products. As a result, enthusiasts can speak to at least some of the visionaries' concerns.

In a comparable way, conservatives look to pragmatists to help lead them in their technology purchases. Both groups like to see themselves as members of a particular industry first, businesspeople second, and purchasers of technology third. Pragmatists, however, have more confidence in technology as a potential benefit and in their ability to make sound technology purchases. Conservatives are considerably more nervous about both. They are willing to go along, up to a point, with pragmatists they respect, but they are still slightly unnerved by pragmatists' overall self-confidence. So, once again, the reference base has partial value in transitioning between adoption segments.

The significance of this weakening in the reference base traces back to the fundamental point made about markets in the introduction: Namely, that markets—particularly high-tech markets—are made up of people who reference each other during the buying decision. As we move from segment to segment in the technology adoption life cycle, we may have any number of references built up, *but they may not be of the right sort.*

Nowhere is this better seen than in the transition between *visionaries* and *pragmatists*. If there are to some extent minor gaps between the other adoption groups, between visionaries and pragmatists there is a great—and to a large extent, greatly ignored—chasm.

If we look deep into that chasm, we see four fundamental characteristics of visionaries that alienate pragmatists.

1. *Lack of respect for the value of colleagues' experiences.* Visionaries are the first people in their industry segment to see the potential of the new technology. Fundamentally, they see themselves as smarter than their opposite numbers in competitive companies—and, quite often, they are. Indeed, it is their ability to see things first that they want to leverage into a competitive advantage. That advantage can only come about if no one else has discovered it. They do not expect, therefore, to be buying a well-tested product with an extensive list of industry references. Indeed, if such a reference base exists, it may actually turn them off, indicating that for this technology, at any rate, they are already too late.

   Pragmatists, on the other hand, deeply value the experience of their colleagues in other companies. When they buy, they expect extensive references, and they want a good number to come from companies in their own industry segment. This, as we have already noted, creates a catch-22 situation; since there are usually only one or two visionaries per industry segment, how can you accumulate the number of references a pragmatist requires, when virtually everyone left to call on is also a pragmatist?

2. *Taking a greater interest in technology than in their industry.* Visionaries are defining the future. You meet them at technology conferences and other futurist forums where people gather to forecast trends and seek out new market opportunities. They are easy to strike up a conversation with, and they understand and appreciate what high-tech companies and high-tech products are trying to do. They want to talk ideas with bright people. They are bored with the mundane details of their own industries. They like to talk and think high tech.

   Pragmatists, on the other hand, don't put a lot of stake in futuristic things. They see themselves more in present-day terms, as the people devoted to making the wheels of their industry turn. Therefore, they tend to invest their convention time in industry-specific forums discussing industry-specific issues. Where pragmatists are concerned, sweeping changes and global advantages may make for fine speeches, but not much else.

3. *Failing to recognize the importance of existing product infrastructure.* Visionaries are building systems from the ground up. They are incarnating their vision. They do not expect to find components for these systems lying around. They do not expect standards to have been established—indeed, they are planning to set new standards. They do not expect support groups to be in place, procedures to have been established, or third parties to be available to share in the workload and the responsibility.

Pragmatists expect all these things. When they see visionaries going their own route with little or no thought of connecting with the mainstream practices in their industry, they shudder. Pragmatists have based their careers on such connections. Once again, it is painfully obvious that visionaries, as a group, make a very poor reference base for pragmatists.

4. *Overall disruptiveness.* From a pragmatist's point of view, visionaries are the people who come in and soak up all the budget for their pet projects. If the project is a success, they take all the credit, while the pragmatists get stuck trying to maintain a system that is so "state-of-the-art" no one is quite sure how to keep it working. If the project fails, visionaries always seem to be a step ahead of the disaster, getting out of town while they can, and leaving the pragmatists to clean up the mess.

Visionaries, successful or not, don't plan to stick around long. They see themselves on a fast track that has them leapfrogging up the corporate ladder and across corporations. Pragmatists, on the other hand, tend to be committed long term to their profession and the company at which they work. They are very cautious about grandiose schemes because they know they will have to live with the results.

All in all, it is easy to see why pragmatists are not anxious to reference visionaries in their buying decisions. Hence the chasm. This situation can be further complicated if the high-tech company, fresh from its marketing successes with visionaries, neglects to change its sales pitch. Thus, the company may be trumpeting its recent success at early test sites when what the pragmatist really wants to hear about are up-and-running production installations. Or the company may be saying "state-of-the-art" when the pragmatist wants to hear "industry standard."

The problem goes beyond pitches and positioning, though. It is fundamentally a problem of time. The high-tech vendor wants—indeed, needs—the pragmatist to buy now, and the pragmatist needs—or at least wants—to wait. Both have absolutely legitimate positions. The fact remains, however, that somewhere a clock has been started, and the question is, who is going to blink first?

For everyone's sake, it had better be the pragmatist. How to make sure of this outcome is the subject of the next section.

PART II

CROSSING THE CHASM

3

The D-Day Analogy

The chasm is, by any measure, a very bad place to be. It promises few, if any, new customers—only those who have somehow got off the safe thoroughfares. But it does house all sorts of unpleasant folk, from disenchanted current customers to nasty competitors to unsavory investors. Their efforts conspire to tax the reserves of the fledgling enterprise seeking to pass through to the mainstream. We need to look briefly at these challenges so we can be alert in our defenses against them.

The Perils of the Chasm

Let's begin with the lack of new customers. As opportunities from the early market of visionaries become increasingly saturated (with big-ticket products this can be after as few as 5 to 10 contracts), and with the mainstream market of pragmatists nowhere near the comfort level they need in order to buy, there is simply an insufficient marketplace of available dollars to sustain the firm. Having flirted with going cash-flow positive (especially during the months following one of the early market big orders), the trend is now reversed, and the enterprise is accelerating into increasingly negative cash flow. Worse still, mainstream competitors, who up to this time had paid no attention to the fledgling entry into their market, now have caught sight of a new target, experienced one or two major losses, and set their sales forces in motion to counterattack.

There are few opportunities for refuge. Managers would like to retreat into their existing major-account relationships, service them in an exceptional way, and leverage that investment of an additional year in fleshing out the greater part of the visionary's plan. This would not only ensure a secured reference base but also begin to create the infrastructure of ancillary products and interfaces needed to turn a discontinuous innovation into the pragmatist's idea of a real-world solution. Unfortunately, there are no extra dollars in these accounts to pay for this year. Indeed, this year of work is far more likely to be necessary just to catch up to the promises made to secure the deal in the first place. So, while there is plenty of good work to do, there is no money here.

Nor can managers find safety through continuing to service just the early market. To be sure, there are still sales opportunities here—other visionaries who can be sold to. But each one is going to have a unique dream, leading to unique demands for customization, which in turn will overtax an already burdened product development group. Moreover, sooner or later in this early market, yet another entrepreneur with a yet more innovative technology, and with a yet better story to tell, will come along. By then you have to be across the chasm and established in the mainstream, or you are out of luck.

There is still more peril. The marketing efforts to date have been funded by investors—either formally, as in the case of venture-funded enterprises, or informally, as is the case with new products developed within larger corporations. These investors have seen some early successes and now expect to see real progress against the business plan's long-term revenue growth objectives. As we now know, seeking this kind of growth during the chasm period is futile. Nonetheless, it is the commitment in the plan (if the commitment had not been made, the funding would not have been available) and the clock is ticking.

Indeed, a truly predatory type of investor—sometimes referred to as a *vulture capitalist*—looks to use the chasm period of struggle and failure as a means to discredit the current management, thereby driving down the equity value in the company, so that in the next round of funding, he or she has an opportunity to secure dominant control of the company, install a new management team, and, worst case, become the owner of a major technology asset, dirt cheap. This is an incredibly destructive exercise during which not only the baby and the bathwater but all human values and winning opportunities are thrown out the window. Nonetheless, it happens.

Even investors with reasonable demands and a supportive attitude, however, can be troubled by the chasm. Under the best-case scenario, you are asking them to rein back their expectations just when it seems most natural to let them fly. There is an underlying feeling that somehow, somewhere, someone has failed. They may be willing to give you the benefit of the doubt for a time, but you don't have any time to waste. You must get into a mainstream market segment soon, establishing long-term relationships with pragmatist buyers, for only through these can you control your own destiny.

Fighting Your Way into the Mainstream

To enter the mainstream market is an act of aggression. The companies who have already established relationships with your target customer will resent your intrusion and do everything they can to shut you out. The customers themselves will be suspicious of you as a new and untried player in their marketplace. No one wants your presence. You are an invader.

This is not a time to focus on being nice. As we have already said, the perils of the chasm make this a life-or-death situation for you. You must win entry to the mainstream, despite whatever resistance is posed. So, if we are going to be warlike, we might as well be so explicitly. For guidance, we are going to look back to an event in the first half of this century, the Allied invasion of Normandy on D Day, June 6, 1944. To be sure, there are more current examples of military success, but this particular analogy relates to our specific concerns very well.

The comparison is straightforward enough. Our long-term goal is to enter and take control of a mainstream market (Eisenhower's Europe) that is currently dominated by an entrenched competitor (the Axis). For our product to wrest the mainstream market from this competitor, we must assemble an invasion force comprising other products and companies (the Allies). By way of entry into this market, our immediate goal is to transition from an early market base (England) to a strategic target market segment in the mainstream (the beaches at Normandy). Separating us from our goal is the chasm (the English Channel). We are going to cross that chasm as fast as we can with an invasion force focused directly and exclusively on the point of attack (D Day). Once we force the competitor out of our targeted niche markets (secure the beachhead), then we will move out to take over additional market segments (districts of France) on the way toward overall market domination (the liberation of Europe).

That's it. That's the strategy. Replicate D Day, and win entry to the mainstream. Cross the chasm by targeting a very specific niche market where you can dominate from the outset, force your competitors out of that market niche, and then use it as a base for broader operations. Concentrate an overwhelmingly superior force on a highly focused target. It worked in 1944 for the Allies, and it has worked since for any number of high-tech companies.

The key to the Normandy advantage, what allows the fledgling enterprise to win over pragmatist customers in advance of broader market acceptance, is focusing an overabundance of support into a confined market niche. By simplifying the initial challenge, the enterprise can efficiently develop a solid base of references, collateral, and internal procedures and documentation by virtue of a restricted set of market variables. The efficiency of the marketing process, at this point, is a function of the "boundedness" of the market segment being addressed. The more tightly bound it is, the easier it is to create and introduce messages into it, and the faster these messages travel by word of mouth.

Companies just starting out, as well as any marketing program operating with scarce resources must operate in a tightly bound market to be competitive. Otherwise their "hot" marketing messages get diffused too early, the chain reaction of word-of-mouth communication dies out, and the sales force is back to selling "cold." This is a classic chasm symptom, as the enterprise leaves behind the niche represented by the early market. It is usually interpreted as a letdown in the sales force or a cooling off in demand when, in fact, it is simply the consequence of trying to expand into too loosely bounded a market.

The D-Day strategy prevents this mistake. It has the ability to galvanize an entire enterprise by focusing it on a highly specific goal that is (1) readily achievable and (2) capable of being directly leveraged into long-term success. Most companies fail to cross the chasm because, confronted with the immensity of opportunity represented by a mainstream market, they lose their focus, chasing every opportunity that presents itself, but finding themselves unable to deliver a salable proposition to any true pragmatist buyer. The D-Day strategy keeps everyone on point—if we don't take Normandy, we don't have to worry about how we're going to take Paris. And by focusing our entire might on such a small territory, we greatly increase our odds of immediate success.

Unfortunately, sound as this strategy is, it is counterintuitive to the management of start-up enterprises, and thus, although widely acknowledged in theory, it is rarely put into practice. Here's the more common scenario.

How to Start a Fire

Starting a fire is a problem that any Boy Scout or Girl Scout can solve. You lay down some bunched-up newspaper, put on some kindling and some logs, and then light the paper. Nothing could be easier. *Trying to cross the chasm without taking a niche market approach is like trying to light a fire without kindling.*

The bunched-up paper represents your promotional budget, and the log, a major market opportunity. No matter how much paper you put under that log, if you don't have any target market segments to act as kindling, sooner or later, the paper will be all used up, and the log still won't be burning. When the pen-based computer came out, companies like Go and Momenta burned their way through tens of millions of dollars in marketing to absolutely no avail. This was a very expensive lesson in scouting.

This isn't rocket science, but it does represent a kind of discipline. And it is here that high-tech management shows itself most lacking. Most high-tech leaders, when it comes down to making marketing choices, will continue to shy away from making niche commitments, regardless. Like marriage-averse bachelors, they may nod in all the right places and say all the right things, but they will not show up when the wedding bells chime. Why not?

First, let us understand that this is a failure of will, not of understanding. That is, it is not that these leaders need to learn about niche marketing. MBA marketing curricula of the past 25 years have been adamant about the need to segment markets and the advantages gained thereby. No one, therefore, can or does plead ignorance. Instead, the claim is made that, although niche strategy is generally best, we do not have time—or we cannot afford—to implement it now. This is a ruse, of course, the true answer being much simpler: *We do not have, nor are we willing to adopt, any discipline that would ever require us to stop pursuing any sale at any time for any reason.* We are, in other words, not a market-driven company; we are a sales-driven company.

Now, how bad can this really be? I mean, sales are good, right? Surely things can just work themselves out, and we will discover our market, albeit retroactively, led to it by our customers, yes? The true answers to the previous three questions are: (1) disastrous, (2) not always, and (3) never in a million years.

The consequences of being sales-driven during the chasm period are, to put it simply, fatal. Here's why: The sole goal of the company during this stage of market development must be to secure a beachhead in a mainstream market—that is, to create a pragmatist customer base that is referenceable, people who can, in turn, provide us access to other mainstream prospects. To capture this reference base, we must ensure that our first set of customers completely satisfy their buying objectives. To do that, we must ensure that the customer gets not just the product but what we will describe in a later chapter as the whole product—the complete set of products and services needed to achieve the desired result. Whenever anything is left out from this set, the solution is incomplete, the selling promise unfulfilled, and the customer unavailable for referencing. Therefore, to secure these much-needed references, which is our prime goal in crossing the chasm, we must commit ourselves to providing, or at least guaranteeing the provision of, the whole product.

Whole product commitments, however, are expensive. Even when we recruit partners and allies to help fulfill them, they require resource-intensive management. And when the support role falls back on us, it often requires the attention of our most key people, the same people who are critical to every other project we have going. Therefore, whole product commitments must be made not only sparingly but strategically—that is, made with a view toward leveraging them over multiple sales. This can only happen if the sales effort is focused on one or two niche markets. More than that, and you burn out your key resources, falter on the quality of your whole product commitment, and prolong your stay in the chasm. To be truly sales-driven is to invite a permanent stay.

For reasons of whole product leverage alone, the sales-driven strategy should be avoided. But its siren lure is so strong that additional ammunition against it is warranted. Consider the following. One of the keys in breaking into a new market is to establish a strong word-of-mouth reputation among buyers. Numerous studies have shown that in the high-tech buying process, word of mouth is the number one source of information buyers reference, both at the beginning of the sales cycle, to establish their "long lists," and at the end, when they are paring down their short ones. Now, for word of mouth to develop in any particular marketplace, there must be a critical mass of informed individuals who meet from time to time and, in exchanging views, reinforce the product's or the company's positioning. That's how word of mouth spreads.

Seeding this communications process is expensive, particularly once you leave the early market, which in general can be reached through the technical press and related media, and make the transition into the mainstream market. Pragmatist buyers, as we have already noted, communicate along industry lines or through professional associations. Chemists talk to other chemists, lawyers to other lawyers, insurance executives to other insurance executives, and so one. Winning over one or two customers in each of 5 or 10 different segments—the consequence of taking a sales-driven approach—will create no word-of-mouth effect. Your customers may try to start a conversation about you, but there will be no one there to reinforce it. By contrast, winning four or five customers in one segment will create the desired effect. Thus, the segment-targeting company can expect word-of-mouth leverage early in its crossing-the-chasm marketing effort, whereas the sales-driven company will get it much later, if at all. *This lack of word of mouth, in turn, makes selling the product that much harder, thereby adding to the cost and the unpredictability of sales.*

Finally, there is a third compelling reason to be niche focused when crossing the chasm, which has to do with the need to achieve market leadership. Pragmatist customers want to buy from market leaders. Their motive is simple: whole products grow up around the market-leading products and not around the others. That is, there are many more books about how to use Intuit's Quicken, many more Quicken-compatible programs, many more Quicken templates, many more directly accessible data sources through Quicken, than with Microsoft's Money. The existence of this added-value infrastructure not only enriches the value of the product but also simplifies the task of getting support. Pragmatists are very much aware of this effect. They do not want to get caught owning a 3DO instead of a Sony Playstation, an OS/2 server instead of Windows NT, or a Progress database instead of an Oracle. Therefore, they perhaps unconsciously but nonetheless consistently conspire to install some company or product as the market leader and then do everything in their power to keep them there. One of the main reasons they delay their buying decisions at the beginning of a marketplace— thereby creating the chasm effect—is to help them get a fix on who the leader will be. They don't want to back the wrong one.

Now, by definition, when you are crossing the chasm, you are not a market leader. The question is, How can you accelerate achieving that state? This is a matter of simple mathematics. To be the leader in any given market, you need the largest market share—typically over 50 percent at the beginning of a market, although it may end up to be as little as 30 to 35 percent later on. So, take the sales you expect to generate over any given time period—say the next two years—double that number, and that's the size of market you can expect to dominate. Actually, to be precise, that is the *maximum* size of market, because the calculation assumes that all your sales came from a single market segment. So, if we want market leadership early on—and we do, since we know pragmatists tend to buy from market leaders, and our number one marketing goal is to achieve a pragmatist installed base that can be referenced—*the only right strategy is to take a "big fish, small pond" approach.*

Segment. Segment. Segment. One of the other benefits of this approach is that it leads directly to you "owning" a market. That is, you get installed by the pragmatists as the leader, and from then on, they conspire to help keep you there. This means that there are significant barriers to entry for any competitors, regardless of their size or the added features they have in their product. Mainstream customers will, to be sure, complain about your lack of features and insist you upgrade to meet the competition. But, in truth, mainstream customers like to be "owned"—it simplifies their buying decisions, improves the quality and lowers the cost of whole product ownership, and provides security that the vendor is here to stay. They demand attention, but they are on your side. As a result, an owned market can take on some of the characteristics of an annuity—a building block in good times, and a place of refuge in bad—with far more predictable revenues and far lower cost of sales than can otherwise be achieved.

For all these reasons—for whole product leverage, for word-of-mouth effectiveness, and for perceived market leadership—it is critical that, when crossing the chasm, you focus exclusively on achieving a dominant position in one or two narrowly bounded market segments. If you do not commit fully to this goal, the odds are overwhelmingly against your ever arriving in the mainstream market.

What About Microsoft?

Let me admit from the outset that, to the best of my knowledge, Microsoft has never followed the niche strategy that I have been so strongly advocating. It has not been a practitioner of the D-Day approach. Instead, it has continually taken what might be called the "Evel Knievel approach": Ignore the chasm. So how in the world has it been so successful, and why wouldn't anybody with a grain of sense follow their model, Mr. Moore, instead of yours?

Here I think we have an example of the legal profession's notion that great cases make bad law. Microsoft's history is so unique it makes it virtually unusable as a precedent for strategy decisions in other companies. All three of its primary technologies—Windows, NT, and Internet Explorer—have been direct extensions of a PC operating system franchise that Microsoft inherited and then stole from IBM. That act of theft was Promethean—the stealing of fire from the gods and giving it to humans.

It was not dishonest, it was brilliant. But the key point here is, Microsoft from day one was operating in a context of being a de facto standard. It was born inside a tornado of demand that IBM created, and all its subsequent acts of market development have been based on being the rich heir to that estate.

That status has allowed Microsoft to coopt new technologies rather than have to introduce them directly. Its success, in other words, has been based primarily on being a fast-follower of technologies introduced first by others. This is clearly true both for Windows, which was derived directly from the Macintosh, and the Internet Explorer, derived directly from Netscape Navigator. And I think the same could be argued for Windows NT whose claim to fame is not that it pushes the state of the art of operating systems forward but rather that it is a truly common standard platform, the real fulfillment of the empty promise of Unix.

The point here is not to deride Microsoft's technological skills but rather to celebrate its market development strategy. As owner of all the clients in a client/server world, it has a permanent enclave on the pragmatist side of the chasm. It controls the gates to the city. When barbarians show up with their discontinuous innovations, it can shut the gates. When it shows up with its own versions of same, it can open the gates. It's Gates' gates, and it is a very lucrative franchise indeed.

What it is not is a good precedent for the rest of us. Whereas Microsoft can work both sides of the chasm, as it were, most other companies have to cross without help. Indeed, often they have to cross in the teeth of Microsoft's resistance. Entering the mainstream market is an act of burglary, of breaking and entering, of deception, often even of stealth. Mapping out a global assault plan, attacking on all fronts at once, may work for massively intimidating market leaders who already have troops in place throughout the world, but it is just plain silly for stripling challengers. Instead, we need to pick our spots carefully, attack fiercely, and then dig in and hold.

Beyond Niches

Now, having said all that, we need also to acknowledge that there is life after niche. Major market dominance ultimately transcends niche, although it continues to renew and extend itself by developing new segments. And this is indeed when the truly large profits are made. It is clearly a postchasm phenomenon, but there is a planning exercise to be done from the outset. Just as the *objective* of D Day was to take Normandy beaches but the *goal* was to liberate France, so in our marketing strategy we want to establish a longer-term vision to guide our immediate tactical choices.

The key to moving beyond one's initial target niche is to select *strategic* target market segments to begin with. That is, target a segment that, by virtue of its other connections, creates an entry point into a larger segment. For example, when the Macintosh crossed the chasm, the target niche was the graphics arts department in Fortune 500 companies. This was not a particularly large target market, but it was one that was responsible for a broken, mission-critical process—providing presentations for executives and marketing professionals. The fact that the segment was relatively small turned out to be good news because Apple was able to dominate it quickly and establish its proprietary system as a legitimate standard within the corporation (against the wishes of the MIS department which wanted everyone on an IBM PC). More importantly, however, having dominated this niche, the company was then able to leverage its win into adjacent departments within the corporation—first marketing, then sales. The marketing people found that if they made their own presentations they could update them on the way to the trade shows, and the salespeople found that with a Mac they didn't have to rely on the marketing people. At the same time, this beachhead in graphics arts also extended out into external markets that interfaced with the graphics arts people—creative agencies, advertising agencies, and eventually, publishers. All used the Macintosh to exchange a variety of graphic materials, and the result was a complete ecosystem standardized on the "non-standard" platform.

How to ensure that one selects a strategic niche for the D-Day landing site is the subject of the next chapter. Before moving on to it, however, let's take a look at some highly visible companies who successfully implemented a highly focused approach to crossing the chasm.

Successful Chasm Crossings[1]

In the paragraphs that follow we will look at four successful chasm crossings—two by applications vendors—Clarify and Documentum—and two by platform vendors—PalmPilot and NEON (New Era of Networks). All four fought off major competition to gain dominant shares of mainstream market niches, and each was able to parlay that into strong equity returns for its investors. But the challenges for platform companies, we shall see, are very different than those facing application companies.

Applications are "naturally vertical" because they directly interface with end users, and end users organize themselves by geography, industry, and profession. This makes them readily adaptable to the beachhead focus needed to cross the chasm. Later on in the life cycle, however, as solutions generalize, mass marketing rewards more of a one-size-fits-all offer, but being tied to end users makes this much harder for an application offer to support.

By contrast, platforms have just the opposite dynamic. They are "naturally horizontal," because they interface with machines and other programs where the value, in part, is providing a stable, standard interface. They do not lend themselves to vertical marketing because, as products, they do not change very much from niche to niche. Unfortunately, however, pragmatist customers rarely adopt any new technology *en masse*. Usually these innovations are taken up first by a single niche, one that has such pressing problems it goes ahead of the herd. The rest of the herd is delighted by the eventuality because it gets a free look at how well the technology plays out without having to take any immediate risk. The niche wins—presuming the beachhead strategy is conducted correctly—by getting a fix for its specialized problem. And the vendor wins because it gets certified by at least one group of pragmatists that its offering is mainstream. So, *because*

---

[1]This is one of two sections in this book that has been significantly rewritten from the ground up. In the original, I made a distinction between two forms of niche marketing—application niches and thematic niches. Subsequent experience proved that there was no such thing as a thematic niche. Instead, the idea anticipated what I came to call the tornado, a mass-market phase of the Technology Adoption Life Cycle that follows the bowling alley and which became the subject of my second book, *Inside the Tornado*.

of the dynamics of technology adoption, and not because of any niche properties in the product itself, platforms must take a vertical market approach to crossing the chasm even though it seems unnatural. The good news for them is that, later on, when a mass market emerges, it is much easier for the platform vendor to take advantage of the opportunity.

Clarify: A Customer Service Application Crosses the Chasm

In the early 1990s, as client/server architecture was crossing the chasm, Clarify developed its flagship application, Clear Support, a software system to improve the productivity of customer service representatives working over the phone. The product was unusual in that it built a picture of each customer interaction around the intersection of three elements: the customer calling, the product that caused the call, and the knowledge that had to be pulled together to solve the customer's problem. This allowed companies using the product to track their customer relationships, identify their problem products, and capture the trouble-shooting learning for reuse in future calls. The customer's problem was assured high visibility by the device of a trouble ticket or "case" that was routed and tracked through the organization until the complaint was resolved. It was—and indeed still is—a great idea, but it required not only new software and significant systems reengineering but also new workflows and new job descriptions, and pragmatists were leery of jumping on board.

There were, however, visionaries who saw in the system a chance to gain a competitive advantage through more responsive service transactions and the opportunity to build long-term relationships with valued customers. The earliest adopters were network hardware systems vendors whose customers always had major challenges during systems integration. Another early adopting segment was medical equipment vendors where the complexity of installation again drove service demands beyond what a normal process could handle. Then there were customers in financial services, offering call centers to their high-net-worth customers, and others in telecommunications, handling complaints and dispatching field service representatives, and still others in high tech, helping their customers and resellers work through all the complexities and bugs in their new products.

One of these last was Cisco Systems, which was emerging at that time as a major player in the network hardware market. Their implementation caught the attention both of their customers and their competitors. Everyone in the industry—vendors, resellers, and customers—were struggling with the increasing severity of the customer support problem, in part because systems in themselves were becoming more complex and in part because they began to interoperate more and more with other systems, creating even more complexity. The market was exploding, and lack of customer support threatened to become a bottleneck to growth. People simply could not hire enough support people or train them fast enough. As a result there emerged a niche-wide demand for technology to help solve these problems.

This is an example of how a vertical market with a broken mission-critical process creates an attractive beachhead opportunity. No longer does the market present itself customer by customer—now it presents an opportunity to go after a whole segment, as one. But there is a price to pay here. The segment has specific needs that weren't prioritized, and these priorities at minimum compete with, and sometimes even directly conflict with, the desires of customers in other markets. What is a company to do in this case?

The answer when crossing the chasm is clear: *Make a total commitment to the niche, and then do your best to meet everyone else's needs with whatever resources you have left over.* In the case of Clarify it made a total commitment to the network hardware companies, winning in short order other key market leaders like Wellfleet, 3Com, and Synoptics, which then gave it the credibility to win additional lesser known companies. These customers, first and foremost, wanted case routing that interfaced with their development organizations' bug reporting applications to ensure that bugs were trapped, tagged, and tracked through to elimination. They also wanted knowledge bases that could capture for reuse highly complex technical knowledge. These were two of the key needs that Clarify prioritized above all their other requests to ensure they helped these customers be successful across the niche.

Winning the network hardware niche allowed the company to leverage itself into an adjacent niche, computer software and systems, where it was able to garner major customers like Microsoft. The customer problems here were not quite as complex, but the call volumes were in many cases much higher. Success in computers was subsequently leveraged into telecommunications, where a new demand emerged, the desire to turn a customer service call into a selling opportunity. This led to the emergence of a second product line, called Clear CallCenter. That product, in turn, has proved of real interest to the financial services community.

And so it goes. Winning the beachhead, knocking over the head pin, creates a dynamic of follow-on adoption, opening up new market opportunities, in part from leveraging a solution from one niche to another, in part from word-of-mouth interaction between customers in the adjacent niches. It worked for Clarify, just as it worked for the company to which we will turn next.

Documentum: A Document Management Application Crosses the Chasm

In 1993 when Jeff Miller took over the reins at Documentum, the company, despite inheriting a wealth of document management technology "for free" when it spun out of Xerox, had gone through three straight years of flat revenues in the $2 million range. This is a classic performance for a company whose market is in the chasm. In the year after Jeff came on board, it went to $8 million, then to $25 million, then $45 million (and an IPO), and then $75 million. That is world-class chasm-crossing. What did Jeff and his team do?

Actually, they took the original edition of *Crossing the Chasm* and made it their market development blueprint. Knowing they were in the chasm, and knowing that the key for first key to getting out was to select a beachhead market segment, they surveyed their client experience to date and targeted a very thin market niche: the regulatory affairs department in Fortune 500 pharmaceutical companies. Now there are only about forty of these in the whole world, and the largest is a few dozen people or so, so how could a company justify reducing its market scope from "all personnel who touch complex documents in all large enterprises," to maybe one thousand people total on the planet?

The answer is that when you are picking a chasm-crossing target it is not about the number of people involved, it is about the amount of pain they are causing. In the case of the pharmaceutical industry's regulatory affairs function, the pain was excruciating. This is the group that has to get the New Drug Approval applications submitted to the 100 or so different regulatory bodies around the world. The process does not start until patents are awarded. The patents have a 17 year life, and a successful patented drug generates on average about $400 million per year. Once the drug goes off patent, however, its economic returns plummet. Every day spent in the application process is a day of patent-life wasted. Pharmaceutical companies were taking up to one year to get their first application filed—not a year to get it approved, a year to get it submitted!

That was because applications range from 250 to 500 thousand pages in length, and come from a myriad of sources— clinical trial studies, correspondence, manufacturing databases, the Patent Office, research lab notebooks, and the like. All this material has to be frozen in time as a master copy, against which all subsequent changes in information are posted and tracked. It is a nightmare of a problem, and it was costing the drug companies big bucks.

By tackling this problem, Documentum ensured itself of a strongly committed customer. The commitment did not come from the IT organization, which *pragmatically* was content to work with its established vendors, making continuous improvements to the existing document management infrastructure. Instead, it came from the top brass who, seeing in Documentum a chance to reengineer the entire process to a very different new end, overruled the in-house folks and demanded that they support the new paradigm. This is a standard pattern in crossing the chasm. It is normally the departmental function who leads (they have the problem), the executive function who prioritizes (the problem is causing enterprise-wide grief), and the technical function that follows (they have to make the new stuff work while still maintaining all the old stuff).

In a year Documentum had demonstrated that it could solve this problem, and some thirty of the top forty companies had committed to its solution. That is what drove its sales to $8 million and then to $25 million. But the revenue since then has come from the bowling-pin effect of niche marketing. Inside the drug companies, Documentum became the standard for all document management tasks, so it spread from the regulatory affairs group to the researchers to the manufacturing floor. Once it got to the floor, the plant construction and maintenance contractors, who were using it to assemble and maintain documentation on all the systems and procedures in the factory, recognized that factories in related process industries had the same needs, and they took the product into regulated chemicals, non-regulated chemicals, and oil refineries. When the product hit the refineries, what people in the oil industry call the downstream part of their business, the IT people recognized a tool that could solve a major problem in their upstream business, exploration and production. There a key concern is the management of leasable properties, what's available, what's under contract, who else is involved, et cetera. It is a rat's nest of interrelated contingencies, and without a document management system, it was being managed largely by word-of-mouth and paper files. Enter Documentum for another major success. And then that success caught the attention of Wall Street, who saw that the same facilities would help them get better control over their swaps and derivatives business.

And that is pretty much the chain of events that had taken Documentum to over $100 million in revenues. It is niche marketing at its most leveraged. There are two keys to this entire sequence. The first is knocking over the head pin, taking the beachhead, crossing the chasm. The size of the first pin is not the issue, but the economic value of the problem it fixes is. The more serious the problem, the faster the target niche will pull you out of the chasm. Once out, your opportunities to expand into other niches are immensely increased because now, having one set of customers solidly behind you, you are much less risky to back as a new vendor.

The second key is to have lined up other market segments into which you can leverage your initial niche solution. This allows you to reinterpret the financial gain in crossing the chasm. It is not about the money you make from the first niche: It is the sum of that money plus the gains from all subsequent niches. It is a bowling alley estimate, not just a head pin estimate, that should drive the calculation of gain. This is a particularly important point for entrepreneurs working inside large corporations who are having to compete for funding against larger, more established market opportunities. If the executive council cannot see the extended market, if they only see the first niche, they won't fund. Conversely, if you go the other way, and show them only an aggregated mass market, the end result of the market going horizontal and into hypergrowth, they will fund, but then they will fire you as you fail to generate these spectacular numbers quickly. The bowling pin model allows you both to focus on the immediate market, keeping the burn rate down and the market development effort targeted, while still keeping in view the larger win.

3Com PalmPilot: A Standalone Platform Crosses the Chasm

Usually when companies struggle with crossing the chasm, it stems from the inability to call out and commit to a single target customer. After all, sales are tight, and restricting the field seems counter-intuitive at best. But occasionally, the target customer has already been picked, and still the industry flails about. This was the case when it came to the PDA (Personal Digital Assistant) market, which struggled for a number of years in the chasm before Palm computing (later acquired by U.S. Robotics, later acquired by 3Com) came out with the PalmPilot and brought the category into the mainstream market. What did they do right that everyone else before them did wrong?

The beachhead target market for PDAs was the management team of high-tech enterprises, who spend 100% of their time either in meetings or on the road. In both situations they need support for contact applications (telephone and email) and for setting up more meetings (calendar). Paper systems have lots of pluses here, but a huge downside in being hard to update and hard to coordinate among individuals. Software can solve the first problem easily and the second problem with difficulty. Given that the target market is predisposed to high tech, there is definitely a compelling reason to buy.

The first wave of entrants into this market came from the consumer electronics space—the Sharp Wizard and the Casio Boss. These products were priced right but were too limited in functionality. They had no calendars at all, and their phone books initially were manual input only, with no back-up. You only had to lose one to never play that game again. This led the market to look toward a more PC-oriented solution. The market had already seen palmtop PCs from Psion and Poquet, neither of which had won enough adherents to be interesting. The next wave of offers came from two major PC players—Hewlett-Packard, with its LX line of palmtop computers, and Apple, with its Newton. Each had a clear shot at the market, and each organization missed. How they missed is particularly instructive.

HP could not let go of the PC. The 95LX had a phone list and a calendar that met a first approximation of the market requirements. Its problem was that it also ran DOS, Lotus 1-2-3, and a word processor. It had a full keyboard, provided you had fingers no broader than a pencil, and PCMCIA slots, and RAM, and, and, and. And it also cost $695. In sum it was neither fish nor fowl, and the market—other than HP employees—said no thank you.

Newton was never a PC. Apple's problem was they could not let go of the vision. John Sculley had sponsored the Knowledge Navigator vision in a compelling video that had everybody's enthusiastic buy-in. Newton was held hostage to that video. A knowledge navigator it wasn't, however—and more importantly, no one was asking to buy such a thing anyway. As a palmtop Newton also met the minimum spec for phonebook and calendaring applications. But its form factor simply was too far off of spec (it was a more like a brick than a deck of cards). Moreover, coordinating calendars in a Microsoft world was not on. But most importantly, it had hyped its pen recognition software which performed so badly in the real world it became the subject of a series of Doonesbury cartoons.

The PalmPilot team, headed by Jeff Hawkins on the technical side and Donna Dublinsky on the business side, had the advantage of seeing a lot of things not work. But to their credit they had the gumption to pick a focus and stick to it. The result was a truly compelling consumer product. The form factor fit in a breast pocket (obsoleting the pocket protector whose space and role it preempted). The application interface was intuitive to anyone who had ever used a Mac or Windows PC (the entirety of the target market), it had a hugely convenient docking station that facilitated upload/download to manage phone numbers and held out the promise of coordinating calendars (the world needed first to decide what calendaring system it would standardize on and then develop the behaviors and processes to support the effort—a work that is still in progress). It used a pen in a way that was restricted enough to actually work. And it met the consumer pricepoint of being under $400. And that was it.

People loved this thing. The technology industry management teams took the lead on it, but pretty quickly it was getting passed around to "the rest of us," and the passion did not abate. It is one of the few products after the Mac that has been able to create passion among a broad class of users. Why? Because it just nailed the problem these folks have. Success through subtraction is the key lesson here. And that subtraction was made possible by a vote of confidence in design esthetics and in target marketing. By contrast, the companies who failed had overdesigned for the target market because they were hedging their bets. Ironically, in the act of trying to reduce their market risk, they actually increased it.

Companies who cannot commit to a single chasm-crossing target almost always fall prey to this mistake. For application companies making this commitment is hard, but for platform companies it is even harder. Platforms by their very nature pay off when they achieve ubiquity, and typically not before. So the investors are rarely enthusiastic about any niche strategy. Moreover, the R&D folks, looking ahead to the full charter, start to build in placeholders for the full array of supported features. And the sales folks, surveying the early opportunities, and liking to have their own turf, each march off in separate directions. It's a huge challenge to manage.

The PalmPilot has subsequently converted itself from a closed appliance, like the Macintosh, to an open platform, like the PC, which the company calls the Palm III. It is doing so under relentless attack from Microsoft's Windows CE platform, which has launched a Palm PC directly at its flagship offer. The Palm III, for example, has incorporated wireless modems and software programs to enable email and Internet access applications, and the company is actively recruiting developers to extend it further. Here their Java Software Development Kit and their support for a PC-standard serial port interface should help a great deal. Moreover, there are "convergence" offers emerging including the melding of a Palm III with a cell phone. Nonetheless, this is a game that Microsoft plays exceptionally well, and gaining ubiquity when playing against an entrenched incumbent is painfully hard. Moreover, increased focus on the platform adds complexity to the delivered system, thereby detracting from the original value proposition. This is OK for advanced PalmPilot users but bad for new ones.

And so the company has also released a Palm V which celebrates the initial vision by being even thinner and sleeker! This jewel even won over a die-hard conservative like myself. By splitting the product line, Palm is able to explore two avenues at once. It is beyond the scope of this book to talk about post-chasm market development (for that the reader is referred to a sequel, *Inside the Tornado*). But we will have occasion to comment further on its challenges after we take a look at one more platform play.

SmartCards: A Distributed Platform Crosses the Chasm

Remember when VCRs came on the market? (OK, I am older than you.) Anyway, the issue then was that VCR manufacturers complained that they would sell more machines if only there were more video tapes to show on them. And the film industry said they would make more video tapes if only there were more machines in circulation to view them. This led to a prolonged period of discomfort, not unlike what happened at the advent of the smartcard.

Smartcards look like credit cards into which have been embedded chips. In the simplest case, these are memory chips which can record cash values along with other identifying information. In more complex forms, they include microprocessors, allowing them, for example, to participate as clients in client/server security applications. All smartcards require a smartcard reader to be activated. Most are contact based (think of an Automated Teller Machine at a bank, although in the United States the cards are all magnetic-strip, not smart), but some are contactless, as in the toll collection systems in, say, Singapore.

Smartcards are a hugely compelling platform to visionaries. Visionary marketers see in them the opportunity to create loyalty programs (frequent flyer miles, frequent shopper cards). Universities see them as a security ID and a debit card. And the Internet community sees them as part of a universal PKI (Public Key Infrastructure) security system. All these applications require smart-card readers, and there is no end to their uses—*if the readers are ubiquitous.* If, however, the density of readers is sparse, so that a back-up system is also required, then most of the value proposition evaporates. And that—achieving density or critical mass—is the key to crossing the adoption chasm with any platform.

The market leader in smart cards is Gemplus with, as the century comes to a close, something like 80% market share worldwide. Almost none of that share, interestingly, comes from the United States. Why? Well let's look where it does come from and see if we can't see the pattern. The first major take-up of smart cards was in Europe for use with public telephones. It solved a nasty problem in "spare change" for travelers from other countries, and it simplified the maintenance of public phones, but the real coup was that it gave each country's PTT (Public Telephone and Telegraph) a cash float similar to what checking account deposits give to banks. Because the PTT is a closed system, it could be rolled out unilaterally and imposed on consumers, albeit for their benefit.

From telephony, smart cards have evolved into other niches. They are used for video decoders in satellite-distributed subscription TV. They are also used for parking fees, toll collection systems, military base IDs, healthcare cards carrying patient information. Get the pattern? In every case it is a closed community, allowing a central agency to unilaterally impose the structure. This ensures high saturation rapidly, thereby justifying the economics of the new infrastructure.

Now, the United States is the least closed community on the planet, and so it should come as no surprise that its adoption of smartcards lags the rest of the world dramatically. And yet it is the United States, perhaps, that will champion the killer app that will drive smartcards to a whole new level of deployment—the Internet, with its demands for a universal security system. But that would represent ubiquity at its least dense, something that is anathema when you are trying to cross the chasm.

So here is the dilemma. How do you get to universal deployment most rapidly? Chasm-crossing theory says, "Act locally, *then* globally." Begin, that is, with high-security Internet-based applications inside closed communities: corporations, financial trading, civil and military intelligence, healthcare information sharing, and the like. Eschew any reader that is not integrated into a PC—the rest of the world will lead in those applications. One attractive form factor is a card reader embedded in a PCMC/A card, able to leverage the broad deployment of PCMC/A slots. Work the intranet to extranet to Internet pattern that is emerging with so many Worldwide-Web-based applications. That is, begin with an internal set of employees, then incorporate trusted partners, then elite customers, and then move out to broader audiences. Do not go straight to mass deployment: If you try, you will not pass Go, and you will not collect $200.

Applications vs. Platforms

As the previous examples have illustrated, there are different risk/reward trade-offs in chasm-crossing strategies, depending on whether you are marketing an application or a platform that can host other applications. For the actual chasm crossing applications have a huge advantage. That is because disruptive innovations are more likely to be championed by end users than by the technology professionals that operate the current infrastructure. Applications are what an end user sees. They can readily gauge the benefits of them. And if the application fixes a broken, mission-critical business process, they can insist on its deployment in spite of an IT department's reluctance.

Platforms, by contrast, are multi-purpose by definition. They are infrastructure and as such are the domain of the IT community. Charged with maintaining the security, reliability, and performance of the current infrastructure, this group is not quick to adopt disruptive technologies which require widespread reengineering of systems. To accelerate the adoption of platforms, then, vendors must clothe them in applications clothing. That is, they must tie them directly to an application in order to gain the end-user sponsorship necessary to secure a beachhead.

Often this involves seemingly unnatural acts, particularly in the mind of the engineering team who continues point out that a computer cannot tell if the transaction is a real estate sale, a newspaper publication, or a revised will. But the communities sponsoring the technology can. Word-of-mouth corroboration of buying decisions is the key criterion in the pragmatist's adoption process. And since real estate people do not talk to newspaper people, and neither of them cares much to talk to lawyers, you cannot develop word-of-mouth support across them. You must pick one, saturate it, and then move on to the next.

Applications normally lend themselves nicely to this kind of niche by niche market extension. Moreover, in any niche that you have saturated, you are likely to remain the market leader for a long time to come. Pragmatists do not like to switch. But this archipelago progression has a downside. It is much slower than mass market adoption, and so if a mass market does emerge, while you are working your handful of niches, some other player is gaining the rest of the world. This is what happened to Wang with its word processor application once PC-based word processors emerged. It is what happened to Lotus Notes when the Internet emerged. It was what happened to the Macintosh when Windows emerged. It was what happened to Silicon Graphics in the face of Sun and Intel.

When markets go mass, platforms have the advantage. Because they can participate openly in many value chains at the same time, they can be taken up in multiple segments simultaneously. And when they become identified as simply a requirement for doing business, as the fax machine, voicemail, laser printers, and Local Area Networks all were in the 1980s, and as cell phones, laptops, email, and the Internet all have been in the 1990s, then they deploy like lightening. These are the huge wins in high tech. Just understand, they are also the hardest types of technology to get across the chasm.

From Idea to Implementation

It is now time to move from the basic idea of chasm crossing to its actual implementation. In the next four chapters we will break up that challenge into four pieces. First we will look at how to select the point of attack, the place to cross, the beachhead, the head bowling pin. Then we will look at what kind of offer it will take to secure that initial target market, and how we as a fledgling enterprise with limited resources can go about fielding such an offer. Then we will look at the enemy, the forces that seek to throw us back off the beach and back into the chasm, and how we can position ourselves for success. And finally we will look at the selling systems themselves, pricing and distribution, to help us pick the right approach to the market during this particularly vulnerable time.

The critical attitude to maintain in all four of these challenges is that chasm-crossing represents a unique time in your enterprise's history. It is a far cry both from your past, where selling to visionaries was the key to success, and your future, which will be focused on either niche or mass market expansion programs. Between these two stages is a singular moment of transition, the penetration of the mainstream market, an act of burglary, of breaking and entering, that requires special techniques used at no other time in the Technology Adoption Life Cycle.

4

Target the Point of Attack

I don't know who said it—it sounds like the sort of thing that gets attributed to Yogi Berra or to his mentor, Casey Stengel—but in any event, when it comes to crossing the chasm, this saying absolutely holds true: "If you don't know where you are going, you probably aren't going to get there."

The fundamental principle for crossing the chasm is to target a specific niche market as your point of attack and focus all your resources on achieving the dominant leadership position in that segment. In one sense, this is a straightforward market-entry problem, to which the correct approach is well known. First you divide up the universe of possible customers into market segments. Then you evaluate each segment for its attractiveness. After the targets get narrowed down to a very small number, the "finalists," then you develop estimates of such factors as the market niches' size, their accessibility to distribution, and the degree to which they are well defended by competitors. Then you pick one and go after it. What's so hard?

The empirical answer here is, I don't know, but nobody seems to do it very well. That is, it is extremely rare that people come to The Chasm Group with a market segmentation strategy already in hand, and when they do have one, it is usually not one they are very confident about. Now, these are smart people, and a lot of them have been to business school, and they know all about market segmentation—so it is not for lack of intellect or knowledge that their market segmentation strategies suffer. Rather, they suffer from a built-in hesitancy and lack of confidence related to the paralyzing effects of having to make a *high-risk, low data decision*.

A High-Risk, Low-Data Decision

Think about it. We already know that crossing the chasm is a high-risk endeavor, the effort of an unknown and unproven invasion force marching into the camp of some fierce and established competitor. We are either going to get it right, or we are going to lose a substantial portion, perhaps even all, of the equity value in our venture. In sum, there's a lot riding on this kind of decision, and severe punishment for making it badly.

Now, with that in mind, think about having to make what may be the most important marketing decision in the history of your enterprise *with little or no useful hard information*. For since we are trying to pick a target market segment that we have not yet penetrated to any great extent, by definition we also lack experience in that arena. Moreover, since we are introducing a discontinuous innovation into that market, no one has any direct experience with which to predict what will happen. The market we will enter, by definition, will not have experienced our type of product before. And the people who have experienced our product before, the visionaries, are so different in psychographic profile from our new target customers—the pragmatists—that we must be very careful about extrapolating our results to date. We are, in other words, in a high-risk, low-data state.

If you now turn to the established case studies in market segmentation, like as not you will discover they will be based on work done on market share problems *in existing markets*—in other words, work done in situations where there is already a reasonable amount of data to work with. There are precious few paradigms for how to proceed when you cannot examine market share data, indeed cannot even conduct an informed interview with an existing customer of the type you are now seeking to win over. In short, you are on your own.

Now, the biggest mistake one can make in this state is to turn to numeric information as a source of refuge or reassurance. We all know about lies, damned lies, and statistics, but for numeric marketing data we need to open up a whole new class of prevarication. This stuff is like sausage—your appetite for it lessens considerably once you know how it is made. In particular, the kind of market-size forecasts that come out of even the most highly respected firms—the ones that get quoted in the press as showing the bright and promising future for some new technology or product—are, by necessity, rooted in multiple assumptions. Each of these assumptions has enormous impact on the resulting projection, each represents an experienced but nonetheless arbitrary judgment of a particular market analyst, and all are typically well documented in the report, but also typically ignored by anyone who quotes from it. And once a number gets quoted in the press, then God help us—because it has become *real*. You know it is real because pretty soon you see new numbers cropping up, with claims for their legitimacy based on their being derivations of these other "established" numbers.

As you can see, this whole thing is a house of cards. In some contexts, it even has some uses, particularly where financial managers must deal on a macro level with high-tech markets. But it is absolute folly to use such numbers for developing crossing-the-chasm marketing strategies. That would be like using a map of the world to find your way from the Newark airport to the World Trade Center.

And yet, that is what some people try to do. As soon as the numbers get up in a chart—or better yet, a graph—as soon as they thus become blessed with some specious authenticity, they become the drivers in high-risk, low-data situations because these people are so anxious to have data. That's when you hear them saying things like, "It will be a billion-dollar market in 1995. If we only get 5 percent of that market . . ." When you hear that sort of stuff, exit gracefully, holding on to your wallet.

Now, most of the people who come to The Chasm Group are more sophisticated than this. They know the numbers do not provide the answers they need. But that doesn't mean they feel any better about having to make a high-risk, low-data decision—

which means, in effect, they are stymied. It is our job to get them out of this semiparalyzed state and back into action.

The only proper response to this situation is to acknowledge the lack of data as a condition of the process. To be sure, you can fight back against this ignorance by gathering highly focused data yourself. But you cannot expect to transform a low-data situation into a high-data situation quickly. And given that you must act quickly, you need to approach the decision from a different vantage point. You need to understand that *informed intuition*, rather than *analytical reason*, is the most trustworthy decision-making tool to use.

Informed Intuition

Despite our culture's anxiety about relying on nonverbal processes, there are situations in which it is simply more effective to substitute right-brained tactics for left-brained ones. Ask any great athlete, or artist, or charismatic leader—ask any great decision maker. All of them describe a similar process, in which analytical and rational means are used extensively both in preparation for and in review of a central moment of performance. But in the moment itself, the actual decisions are made intuitively. The question is, How can we use this testimony to our advantage in crossing the chasm in a reasonable and predictable way?

The key is to understand how intuition—specifically, *informed intuition*—actually works. Unlike numerical analysis, it does not rely on processing a statistically significant sample of data in order to achieve a given level of confidence. Rather, it involves conclusions based on isolating a few high-quality images—really, data fragments—that it takes to be archetypes of a broader and more complex reality. These images simply stand out from the swarm of mental material that rattles around in our heads. They are the ones that are memorable. So the first rule of working with an image is: If you can't remember it, don't try, because it's not worth it. Or, to put this in the positive form: Only work with memorable images.

Now, just as in literature, where memorable characters like Hamlet or Heathcliff or even Dirty Harry stand out and become symbols for a larger segment of humanity, so in marketing can whole target-customer populations become imagined as teeny-boppers, yuppies, pickups and gun racks, or the man in the gray flannel suit. These are all just images—stand-ins for a greater reality—picked out from a much larger set of candidate images on the grounds that they really "click" with the sum total of an informed person's experience. These were, in short, the memorable ones.

Let us call these images *characterizations*. As such, they represent characteristic market behaviors. Teenyboppers, for example, can be expected to shop at a mall, emulate a rock star, seek peer approval, and resist parental restrictions—all of which imply that certain marketing tactics will be more successful than others in winning over their dollars. Now, *visionaries, pragmatists,* and *conservatives* represent a set of images analogous to teenybopper, yuppie, and so on—albeit at a higher level of abstraction. For each of these labels also represents characteristic market behaviors—specifically, in relation to adopting a discontinuous innovation—from which we can predict the success or failure of marketing tactics. The problem is, they are too abstract. They need to become more concrete, more target-market specific. That is the function of *target-customer characterization*.

Target-Customer Characterization
The Use of Scenarios

First, please note that we are not focusing here on target-*market* characterization. The place most crossing-the-chasm marketing segmentation efforts get into trouble is at the beginning, when they focus on a target market or target segment instead of on a *target customer*.

Markets are impersonal, abstract things: the personal computer market, the one-megabit RAM market, the office automation market, and so on. Neither the names nor the descriptions of markets evoke any memorable images—they do not elicit the cooperation of one's intuitive faculties. We need to work with something that gives more clues about how to proceed. We need something that feels a lot more like real people. However, since we do not have real live customers as yet, we are just going to have to make them up. Then, once we have their images in mind, we can let them guide us to developing a truly responsive approach to their needs.

Target-customer characterization is a formal process for making up these images, getting them out of individual heads and in front of a marketing decision-making group. The idea is to create as many characterizations as possible, one for each different type of customer and application for the product. (It turns out that, as these start to accumulate, they begin to resemble one another so that, somewhere between 20 and 50, you realize you are just repeating the same formulas with minor tweaks, and that in fact you have outlined 8 to 10 distinct alternatives.) Once we have built a basic library of possible target-customer profiles, we can then apply technique to reduce these "data" into a prioritized list of desirable target market segment opportunities. The quotation marks around *data* are key, of course, because we are still operating in a low-data situation. We just have a better set of *material* to work with.

Electronic Books: An Illustrative Example[2]

For the purposes of illustration, let us consider how we might market an electronic book, where content is downloaded over the Internet into a laptop-like device, weighing three pounds, dedicated exclusively to reading. The first two of these products—Softbook and Rocket eBook—were launched in the fall of 1998. Their claim to fame is that you can carry as many books as you want with you, get new books anytime anywhere, search books with the power of a computer, and—well—be the first kid on your block to own an electronic book.

Now, let us suppose that in the first year or so electronic books win over an early market of technology enthusiasts ("Hey, wanna see my cool new e-book?") and visionaries ("With e-books, we can change the way higher education is conducted!"). Amazon.com announced it will support downloads. Some way-cool book author (say, the author formerly known as Tom Clancy) announces his next book will *only* appear in e-form.

---

[2]This is the other section of the book that is significantly revised from the original. In the intervening years The Chasm Group has used the scenario methodology broadly, and what follows reflects a much improved approach.

The Pentagon buys 10,000 units but won't say what for. And Tom Cruise puts an e-book in his next movie. Now it is time to go after the mainstream market, taking market share away from traditional paper-based books. Where would you begin?

This is a classic case of, "So many segments, so little time"— exactly the sort of thing that target-customer scenarios are best for. A representative format for any given scenario is illustrated in the following section. A finished scenario should be limited to a single page. As you will see from the example, this is a highly tactical exercise in microcosm, but it has major implications for how marketing strategy is set overall. So as we work through the example, we will also keep an eye out for the broader implications.

Sample Scenario

1. *Header information.* At the top of the page you need thumbnail information about the end user, the technical buyer, and the economic buyer of the offer. For business markets, the key data are: industry, geography, department, and job title. For consumer markets, they are demographic: age, sex, economic status, social group.

   For our sample scenario, we are going to focus on a maintenance application in aerospace. So our key header information is:

User:	Aerospace, U.S., maintenance department, flight systems specialist
Technical buyer:	IT department, document management applications director
Economic buyer:	Maintenance department, director

   In consumer scenarios, the three roles of user, technical buyer, and economic buyer tend to merge into one or two. If the user is a child, the economic buyer is the parent, and the technical buyer is a toss-up (in our house, the child for sure). If the user is an adult, the economic buyer often is the other spouse (as in, is it OK for me to spend our money on this doodad?), and the technical buyer tends to be the user. One caveat though: It is extremely difficult to cross the chasm in consumer market. Almost all successful crossings happen in business markets, where the economic and technical resources can absorb the challenges of an immature product and service offering.

The idea behind the header information is to focus the marketing and R&D teams on a specific instance of how the product would be bought and used. Do not worry about being overly focused at this point. The devil is always in the details, and these scenarios are all about getting the devil in view.

2. *A Day in the Life (Before)*

The idea here is to describe a situation in which the user is stuck, with significant consequences for the economic buyer. The elements you need to capture are five:

- *Scene or situation:* Focus on the moment of frustration. What is going on? What is the user about to attempt?
- *Desired outcome:* What is the user trying to accomplish? Why is this important?
- *Attempted approach:* Without the new product, how does the user go about the task?
- *Interfering factors:* What goes wrong? How and why does it go wrong?
- *Economic consequences:* So what? What is the impact of the user failing to accomplish the task productively?

Using aircraft maintenance as an example, we might generate the following:

Scene or Situation

Ernie has been called in to find out why the shrevostat light on the aircraft console is blinking red. The plane has boarded and is otherwise ready to depart. As Ernie looks over the dash, he realizes he has never actually worked on a shrevostat before.

Desired outcome:

Everyone would like to get the problem diagnosed quickly. Ideally, it would then be fixed and the plane could get on its way.

Attempted approach:

Ernie calls down to Wally to check out the shrevostat manual. Unfortunately, the last three revisions have not been posted, so Wally has to go search them down. When he gets them, he tries to describe a diagram over the phone to Ernie, which only confuses things. So Wally gets in a truck to drive over.

Interfering factors:

Manuals can only be in one place at one time. Paper manuals are challenging to update accurately and in a timely manner. The volume of materials is such that you can't carry them with you.

Economic consequences:

Flight is canceled. Maintenance crews are taken offline to fix the problem, resulting in overtime and other delays.

3. *A Day in the Life (After)*

Now the idea is to take the same situation, and the same desired outcome, but to replay the scenario with the new technology in place. Here you just need to capture three elements:

- *New approach:* With the new product how does the end user go about the task?
- *Enabling factors:* What is it about the new approach that allows the user to get unstuck and be productive?
- *Economic rewards:* What are the costs avoided or benefits gained?

Staying with the aircraft example, we might generate the following:

New approach:

Ernie pulls out his e-book which contains all documentation for the Boeing 737 E series, searches for shrevostat, finds the section, including the diagram, and the latest revisions, all automatically downloaded each night. There is a hyperlink in the text to a knowledge

base where actual experiences are tracked. Clicking on
it, the e-book connects to the base. Ernie spots the problem in a flash, applies the fix, and the plane is on its way.
(OK, actually the plane is still delayed, and I am still on
it, but that's another story.)

Enabling factors:

E-books can carry essentially unlimited amounts of material. They can be updated electronically, automatically, over the Internet. They can host software tools to
support text and topic searches and the like.

Economic rewards:

Set aside whether the plane flies or not. Cost avoidance
lies primarily in maintenance worker productivity. But
the system might pay for itself in avoided printing and
updating costs.

Processing the Scenario:
The Market Development Strategy Checklist

Target customer characterization is at the core of applying market
segmentation strategy to the problem of crossing the chasm. It
supplies the "data." Assume that we have spent a day with a
group of ten or so field-savvy members of the e-book company
compiling a library of, say, fifty or so of these scenarios. In this
library we have captured scenarios for every current customer,
every interesting prospect whether won, lost, or in waiting, as
well as other interesting prospects which we might know about
from past lives.

This is not a formal segmentation survey—they take too long,
and their output is too dry. Instead, it is a tapping into the fund
of anecdotes that actually carries business knowledge in our culture. Like much that is anecdotal, these scenarios will incorporate
fictions, falsehoods, prejudices, and the like. Nonetheless, they
are by far the most useful and most accurate form of data to work
with at this stage in the segmentation process. Compared to SIC
codes, for example, they are paragons of accuracy and integrity.
Nonetheless, they are still crude at best, and now it is time to
submit them to a refinery—the Market Development Strategy
Checklist.

This list consists of a set of issues around which go-to-market plans are built, each of which incorporates a chasm-crossing factor, as follows:

- Target customer
- Compelling reason to buy
- Whole product
- Partners and allies
- Distribution
- Pricing
- Competition
- Positioning
- Next target customer

Processing the scenarios consists of rating each scenario against each of these issues. The process actually takes place in two stages. In Stage 1, all scenarios are rated against four "showstopper" issues. Low scores in any one of these typically eliminates the scenario from future consideration *as the beachhead segment*. That is, the niche may a good one to pursue after the chasm has been crossed, but it is not a good target for the crossing itself.

Scenarios which pass the first cut are rated against the remaining five factors. At both stages scores are awarded for each factor, and the scenarios are rank ordered by score. At the end of the process, top-ranked scenarios are taken to be the top chasm-crossing targets. They are further discussed until the team commits to one—*and only one*—beachhead target.

The italics immediately above are meant to answer the single most asked question of The Chasm Group: *Can't we go after more than one target?* The simple answer is no. (The more complex answer is also no, but it takes longer to explain.) Just as you cannot hit two balls with one bat swing, hit two birds with one stone, or brush your teeth and your hair at the same time, so you cannot cross the chasm in two places. We've already discussed this, of course, but trust me, one cannot make this point too often.

Turning back to the checklist, the four factors that raise showstopper issues for crossing the chasm are as follows:

Target customer:	Is there a single, identifiable economic buyer for this offer, readily accessible to the sales channel we

intend to use, and sufficiently well-funded to pay the price for the whole product?

In the absence of such a buyer, sales forces waste valuable time evangelizing groups of people trying to generate a sponsor. Sales cycles drag on forever, and the project can be shut down at any time.

Compelling reason to buy: Are the economic consequences sufficient to mandate any reasonable economic buyer to fix the problem called out in the scenario?

If pragmatists can live with the problem for another year, they will. But they will continue to be interested in learning more. So your sales people will be invited back again and again—they just won't return with purchase orders. Instead, they will report that the customer said, "Great presentation!" What the customer was really saying was, "I learned some more and I didn't have to buy anything."

Whole product: Can our company with the help of partners and allies field a complete solution to the target customer's compelling reason to buy in the next three months such that we can be in the market by the end of next quarter and be dominating the market within twelve months thereafter?

The clock is ticking. We need to cross now, which means we need a problem we can solve now. Any thread left hanging could be the one that trips us up.

Competition: Has this problem already been addressed by another company such that they have crossed the chasm ahead of us and occupied the space we would be targeting?

Dick Hackborn, the HP executive who led the move into laser printers, had a favorite saying: "Never attack a fortified hill." Same with beachheads. If some other company got there before you, all the market dynamics that you are seeking to make work in your favor are already working in its favor. Don't go there.

When scenarios are scored against these four factors, 1 to 5, the worst total score they can get is 4, the best a 20, and with higher-rated scenarios preferred. But there is an additional caveat. A very low score, relative to the others, in any of these factors almost always is a show-stopper. So it is not just total score alone that matters. When in doubt, favor scenarios which have a high-rated compelling reason to buy. If they have already attracted a competitor, see if you can't end run them. Expect that the best scenarios will be "whole product challenged"—if it were easy, someone else would have done it. Indeed, the fact that it is hard will create a barrier to entry in your favor once you have stepped up to the solution.

The remaining factors fall into the "nice to have" category. That is, low scores can usually be overcome, given investment and time. Since, however, investment and time are two of your scarcest resources, cheaper and sooner are very desirable attributes in a target market scenario. Here's how they play out:

Partners and allies: Do we already have relationships begun with the other companies needed to fulfill the whole product?

If you do, it is typically from a single early-market project, or else you are just lucky. Pulling together this partnership is a major challenge for the whole product manager.

Distribution: Do we have a sales channel in place that can call on the target customer and fulfill the whole product requirements put on distribution?

Calling on the line-of-business side of the house requires some fluency in the language of the target niche, and established relationships with individuals accelerates this process dramatically. Lacking this, companies typically hire a well-connected individual out of the target industry and charter her to lead the sales force back in.

Pricing: Is the price of the whole product consistent with the target customer's budget and with the value gained by fixing the broken process? Do all the partners, including the distribution channel, get compensated sufficiently to keep their attention and loyalty?

Note here that it is the whole product price, not the price of the product per se, that matters. Services will often take as much or more of this total as product.

Positioning: Is the company credible as a provider of products and services to the target niche?

At the outset, the answer is typically, Not very. One of the delights of niche marketing, however, is the speed at which this resistance can be overcome if only one truly commits to a whole product that fixes the broken process.

Next target customer: If we are successful in dominating this niche, does it have good "bowling pin" potential? That is, will these customers and partners facilitate our entry into adjacent niches?

This is an important issue of strategy. Chasm-crossing is not the end, but rather the beginning, of mainstream market development. It is important that we have additional follow-on niches that can be lucratively addressed. Else the economics of niche marketing simply do not hold up.

After the scenarios that passed the first round of show-stopper screening have been scored on this second set of factors, and then rank ordered by score, the team has extracted all of the "data" this process can provide. It is now time to make the high-risk, low-data decision and get on with it.

Committing to the Point of Attack

Making the commitment to a niche market can be challenging, especially for entrepreneurs who are technology enthusiasts or visionaries, because they personally don't have the pragmatist response and thus have trouble trusting in the market dynamics outlined in this book. This is a defining moment for them. The start-up company must either cross or die, but what value is life if to gain it one has to go against one's best self? Not an easy question to answer.

When faced with such nasty decisions, it is usually best to make them quickly, get into the new flow, and plan to course-correct going forward. This is a white-water rafting strategy, where hesitating on a split decision is the one behavior guaranteed to capsize the boat. When you do pick, you pick hard. That is, you go hard in the direction chosen, regardless of doubts. Just so with crossing the chasm.

The good news in this is that you do not have to pick the optimal beachhead to be successful. What you must do is win the beachhead you have picked. If there is a genuine problem in the segment, you will have the target customer pulling for you. If it is a hard problem, and the segment is reasonably small, you probably will not have competition to distract you. This means you can focus all your attention on the whole product, which is where it needs to be. Nail that and you win.

What could cause you to change course? Most often, it is that the scenario that is driving the effort is based on a false assumption. To guard against this, you should commission some market research early in the process specifically to validate the winning scenario. But you should not wait for this research to be complete before you start forward. The enemy in the chasm is always time. You must force the pace at all times, even when in doubt, because standing still plays into the hands of the established vendors and the status quo.

And Yes, Size Matters

Finally, when you are on the verge of making the commitment to the target segment, sooner or later the issue of how much revenue the segment could generate comes up. At this point, people normally think that bigger is better. In fact, this is almost never the case. Here's why.

To become a going concern, a persistent entity in the market, you need a customer market that will commit to you as its de facto standard for enabling a critical business process. To become that de facto standard, you need to win at least half, and preferably a lot more, of the new orders in the segment over the next year. That is the sort of vendor performance that causes pragmatist customers to sit up and take notice. At the same time, you will still be taking orders from other segments. So do the math.

Suppose you can get half of next year's orders from the target segment—no mean feat considering that, prior to a couple of days ago, you hadn't focused on it at all. Say your revenue target is $10 million over all. That means $5 million from the target segment. It also means that same $5 million has to represent at least half of the total orders from the segment if you are to have the desired market-leader impact. In other words, if you are going to be a $10-million company next year you do not want to attack a segment larger than $10 million. At the same time, it should be large enough to generate your $5 million. So the rule of thumb in crossing the chasm is simple: *Pick on somebody your own size.*

If you find the target segment is too big, subsegment it. But be careful here. You must respect word-of-mouth boundaries. The goal is to become a big fish in a small pond, not one flopping about trying to straddle a couple of mud puddles. The best sub-segmentation is based on special interest groups within the general community. These typically are very tightly networked and normally form because they have very special problems to solve. In the absence of such, geography can often be a safe subsegmentation variable, provided that it affects the way communities congregate.

If the target segment is too small to generate half of next year's sales for the new product, then you have to augment it. Again, be careful to respect genuine segmentation boundaries. If there is no appropriate supersegment, then you probably should go back and pick another target.

Recap: The Target Market Selection Process

We have been saying all along that the material in this chapter and the following three chapters is tactical by nature—that is, made up of relatively specific tasks and exercises that can, and should, be performed recurrently throughout a major enterprise. As a way of recapping this material, at the end of each chapter there will be a checklist of activities, suitable as a means either for managing a group through this process or testing the final output of a group's marketing decision making.

For selecting the target market segment that will serve as the point of entry for crossing the chasm into the mainstream market, the checklist is as follows:

1. Develop a library of target-customer scenarios. Draw from anyone in the company who would like to submit scenarios, but go out of your way to elicit input from people in customer-facing jobs. Keep adding to it until new additions are no more than minor variations on existing scenarios.
2. Appoint a subcommittee to make the target market selec-

tion. Keep it as small as possible but include on it anyone who could veto the outcome.

3. Number and publish the scenarios in typed form, one page per scenario. Accompanying the bundle, provide a spreadsheet with the rating factors assigned to columns and the scenarios assigned to rows. Break the rating factors into two subtotals, showstoppers first, then nice-to-haves.

4. Have each member of the subcommittee privately rate each scenario on the show-stopper factors. Roll up individual ratings into a group rating. During this process discuss any major disagreements about scores. This typically surfaces different points of view on the same scenario and is critical not just to getting the opportunity correctly in focus but also in laying the groundwork for a future consensus that will stick.

5. Rank order the results and set aside scenarios which do not pass the first cut. This is typically about two thirds of the submissions.

6. In a 400 degree oven, bake . . . (Oops! Wrong book. Sorry.) Repeat the private rating and public ranking process on the remaining scenarios with the remaining selection factors. Winnow the scenario population down to, at most, a favored few.

7. Depending on outcome, proceed as follows:

- *Group agrees on beachhead segment.* Go forward on that basis.
- *Group cannot decide among a final few.* Give the assignment to one person to build a bowling pin model of market development, incorporating as many of the final few as is reasonable, and calling out a head pin. Attack the head pin.
- *No scenario survived.* This does happen. In that case, do not attempt to cross the chasm. Also, do not try to grow. Continue to take early-market projects, keep burn rate as low as possible, and continue search for a viable beachhead.

5

Assemble the Invasion Force

"I have always found you get a lot more in this world with a kind word and a gun than you do with just a kind word."

—Willie Sutton

Willie is only restating what any military leader will confirm: If you are committing an act of aggression, you'd better have the force to back it up. Or, to put this in terms closer to our immediate topic, marketing is *warfare*—not *wordfare*.

Which of us, about to launch an invasion, would prefer a good set of slogans to a good set of offensive and defensive weapons? Who would rather buy advertising time on television than missiles and munitions? Who would rather publish a manifesto than have guaranteed treaties with neighboring countries? Most high-tech executives—that's who.

There is a widespread perception among high-tech executives that marketing consists primarily of some long-range strategic thinking (when you can afford to take the time for it) and then a lot of tactical sales support—with nothing in between. In fact, marketing's most powerful contribution happens right in between. It is called *whole product marketing*, a term introduced earlier, and it is the fundamental basis for assembling the invasion force.

Consider the following scenario. When I was a salesman, I had a dream. The dream was simple. There was a monster bid coming up—with a $5 million minimum—and I had *wired* the request for proposal (RFP). I had, in the words of gamblers everywhere, a *mortal lock* on the thing. The client had met with me for long hours of consultation during which he had bought into every selling argument in favor of my product. He had then constructed the RFP so that only my product could get a 100 percent evaluation. The deal was mine. Then I woke up.

Okay—so that's a fantasy. But a version of that fantasy can be executed in the real world. We might call it *wiring the marketplace.* Again, the concept is simple. For a given target customer and a given application, create a marketplace in which your product is the only reasonable buying proposition. That starts, as we saw in the last chapter, with targeting markets that have a *compelling reason to buy* your product. The next step is to ensure that you have a monopoly over fulfilling that reason to buy.

To secure that monopoly, you need to understand (1) what a *whole product* consists of and (2) how to organize a marketplace to provide a whole product incorporating your company's offering.

The Whole Product Concept

One of the most useful marketing constructs to become integrated into high-tech marketing in the past few years is the concept of a whole product, an idea described in detail in Theodore Levitt's *The Marketing Imagination,* and one that plays a significant role in Bill Davidow's *Marketing High Technology.* The concept is very straightforward: There is a gap between the marketing promise made to the customer—the compelling value proposition—and the ability of the shipped product to fulfill that promise. For that gap to be overcome, the product must be augmented by a variety of services and ancillary products to become the whole product.

The formal model is diagramed by Levitt as follows:

The model identifies four different perceptions of product, as follows:

1. *Generic product:* This is what is shipped in the box and what is covered by the purchasing contract.
2. *Expected product:* This is the product that the consumer

The Whole Product Model

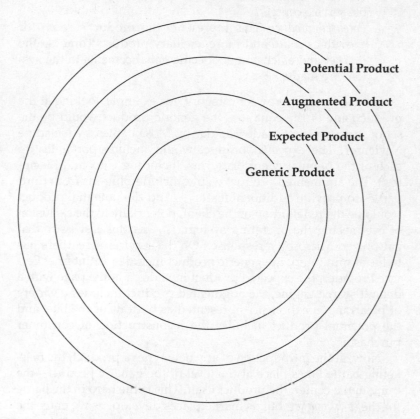

Potential Product

Augmented Product

Expected Product

Generic Product

thought she was buying when she bought the generic product. It is the *minimum* configuration of products and services necessary to have any chance of achieving the buying objective.

For example, people who are buying personal computers for the first time *expect* to get a monitor with their purchase—how else could you use the computer?—but in fact, in most cases, it is not part of the generic product.

3. *Augmented product:* This is the product fleshed out to provide the *maximum* chance of achieving the buying objective. In the case of a personal computer, this would include a variety of products, such as software, a hard disk drive, and a printer, as well as a variety of services, such as a

customer hot line, advanced training, and readily accessible service centers.

4. *Potential product:* This represents the product's room for growth as more and more ancillary products come on the market and as customer-specific enhancements to the system are made.

For the Internet browser category, for example, looking at the product side of the equation, the generic product would be the set of functions first made popular by Mosaic, then by Netscape Navigator. The expected product would include portability to each of the popular client platforms, including Unix and Macintosh. The augmented product would include plug-ins from third parties to provide additional features. And the potential product would be the redefinition of the client, potentially to the exclusion of ever seeing the operating system. (It was this last issue that galvanized Microsoft's response.) On the services side, there has to be, at minimum, the generic product includes an Internet Service Provider, the expected product includes a home page with a default search engine, the augmented product includes a variety of prearranged experiences presented as buttons or the like, and the potential product includes the reconstruction of consumer purchasing.

Now, at the introduction of any new type of product, the marketing battle takes place at the level of the generic product—the thing in the center, the product itself. This is the hero in the battle for the *early market*. But as marketplaces develop, as we enter the *mainstream market*, products in the center become more and more alike, and the battle shifts increasingly to the outer circles. To understand how to dominate a mainstream marketplace we need to take a closer look at the significance of what Paul Harvey might call *the rest of the whole product*.

The Whole Product and the Technology Adoption Life Cycle

First, let's look at how the whole product concept relates to crossing the chasm. If we look at the Technology Adoption Life Cycle as a whole, we can generalize that the outer circles of the whole product increase in importance as one moves from left to right. That is, the customers least in need of whole product support are the technology enthusiasts. They are perfectly used to cobbling together bits and pieces of systems and figuring out their own way to a whole product that pleases them. In fact, this is in large part the pleasure they take from technology products—puzzling through ways to integrate an interesting new capability into something they could actually use. Their motto is: Real techies don't need whole products.

For the visionaries, there is no pleasure in pulling together a whole product on their own, but there is an acceptance that, if they are going to be the first in their industry to implement the new system—and thereby gain a strategic advantage over their competitors—then they are going to have to take responsibility for creating the whole product under their own steam. The rise in interest in systems integration is a direct response to increasing visionary interest in information systems as a source of strategic advantage. Systems integrators could just as easily be called whole product providers—that is their commitment to the customer.

So much for the market to the left of the chasm, the early market. To get to the right of the chasm—to cross into the mainstream market—you have to first meet the demands of the pragmatist customers. These customers want the whole product to be readily available from the outset. They like a product such as Microsoft because there are not only books in every bookstore about how to use it but also seminars for training, office hot-line support, and a whole cadre of temporary office workers already trained on the product. If instead the pragmatists are offered a "great deal" on an alternative product—an office suite from Corel or Lotus, for example—they are not motivated to switch because the rest of the whole product simply cannot match up.

The same logic holds for why pragmatists prefer Intel's microprocessors to Digital's alpha, Windows NT to Linux, Oracle to Sybase, SAP to QAD, Lotus Notes to Novell's Groupwise, Hewlett-Packard printers to Lexmark's, and Sun workstations to Silicon Graphics. In every case, there are strong arguments that they are preferring an inferior product—if you look only at the generic product. But in every case, they are preferring the superior product, if you look at the whole product.

To net this out: Pragmatists evaluate and buy whole products. The generic product, the product you ship, is a key part of the whole product, make no mistake. But once there are more than one or two comparable products in the marketplace, then investing in additional R&D at the generic level has a decreasing return, whereas there is an increasing return from marketing investments at the levels of the expected, the augmented, or the potential product. How to determine where to target these investments is the role of whole product planning.

Whole Product Planning

As we have just seen, the whole product model provides a key insight into the chasm phenomenon. The single most important difference between early markets and mainstream markets is that the former are willing to take responsibility for piecing together the whole product (in return for getting a jump on their competition), whereas the latter are not. Failure to recognize this principle has been the downfall of many a high-tech enterprise. Too often companies throw their products into the market as if they were tossing bales of hay off the back of a truck. There is no planning for the whole product—just the hope that their product will be so wonderful that customers will rise up in legions to demand that third parties rally about it. Well, God did divide the Red Sea for Moses.

For those who wish to take a more prudent course, however, whole product planning is the centerpiece for developing a market domination strategy. Pragmatists will hold off committing their support until they see a strong candidate for leadership emerge. Then they will back that candidate forcefully in an effort to squeeze out the other alternatives, thereby bringing about the necessary standardization to ensure good whole product development in their marketplace.

A good generic product is a great asset in this battle, but it is neither a necessary nor a sufficient cause of victory. Oracle did not have the best product when the market standardized on it. What Oracle offered instead was the best case for a viable whole product—SQL standardization plus broad portability across hardware platforms plus an aggressive sales force to drive product into the market quickly. That is what the pragmatists in MIS got behind.

In short, winning the whole product battle means winning the war. And, because perception contributes to that reality, looking like you are winning the whole product battle is a key weapon to winning the war. On the other hand, *pretending* you are winning the whole product battle is a losing tactic—people check up on each other too much in the high-tech marketplace. These distinctions will become critically important in our next chapter, where we deal with *positioning*.

For now, our focus should be on the minimum commitment to whole product needed to cross the chasm. That is defined by that whole product which assures that the target customers can fulfill their compelling reason to buy. To work out how much whole product this is, you only need a simplified version of the whole model:

The Simplified Whole Product Model

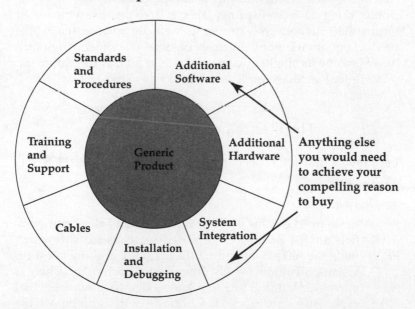

In the simplified model there are only two categories: (1) what we ship and (2) whatever else the customers need in order to achieve their compelling reason to buy. The latter is the *marketing*

promise made to win the sale. The contract does not require the company to deliver on this promise—but the *customer relationship* does. Failure to meet this promise in a business-to-business market has extremely serious consequences. As the bulk of purchases in this marketplace are highly reference oriented, such failure can only create negative word of mouth, causing sales productivity to drop dramatically.

Classically, high tech has delivered 80 to 90 percent of a whole product to any number of possible target customers, but 100 percent to few, if any. Anything less than 100 percent, unfortunately, means that the customers either supply the remainder themselves or feel cheated. Significantly less than 100 percent means that the target market simply does not develop as forecast—even if the generic product, the product in the box being shipped, is superior to anything else in its class.

In short, if you wanted to trace disillusionment with high tech's inability to deliver on its promise to its investors and its customers, lack of attention to whole product marketing is the closest thing to a wellspring. This is actually, great news—it means that the converse applies as well. By solving the whole product equation for any given set of target customers, high tech has overcome its single greatest obstacle to market development.

Let's look at an example to see how this works out.

The Electronic Book, Revisited

Let's revisit the "after" scenario for the electronic book. Here it is again:

New approach:

> Ernie pulls out his e-book which contains all documentation for the Boeing 737 E series, searches for shrevostat, finds the section, including the diagram, and the latest revisions, all automatically downloaded each night. There is a hyperlink in the text to a knowledge base where actual experiences are tracked. Clicking on it, Ernie spots the problem in a flash, applies the fix, and the plane is on its way. (OK, actually the plane is still delayed, and I am still on it, but that's another story.)

Now, let's analyze this scenario in light of its implied whole product commitments. There are several:

- *"Pulls out his e-book."* OK, this is a minor one, but from where? It weighs 3 pounds, remember, and it is breakable. How does Ernie carry this thing around? At minimum, we probably need a case with a strap and we may want a handle on the book itself. In addition, we probably want an industrial strength chassis, but without adding weight.
- *"Which contains all the documentation for the Boeing 737 E."* Oh really? And where did all that documentation come from? Ideally it would be all in one electronic, but in fact there are numerous subcontractors, submitting changes all the time, in file formats different from one another, and from the original itself. Solving this problem is something that specialized document management software like Documentum's addresses. Moreover, it is a major project to populate the database at the outset and takes considerable resources going forward to maintain it.
- *"All automatically downloaded each night."* This implies a docking station for the e-book, or an interface to a PC that serves as such. It implies a raft of IT department procedures to ensure ongoing quality and consistency. It implies sufficient network bandwidth to get the download done in a timely manner. And it implies a connectivity port that can handle high volume (perhaps not the USB port that comes with the standard e-book, but a 1394 "Firewire" port instead).
- *"There is a hyperlink in the text."* Only if someone or something put it there. This, in turn, implies an indexing effort, either manual or through some form of artificial intelligence engine.
- *"To a knowledge base where actual experiences are tracked."* This implies a customer support system such as those supplied by Clarify, Vantive, Seibel, and others. It also implies a programmed interface between that system and the e-book.
- *"Clicking on it."* Well, if the clicking is going to do anything, we just added some sort of wireless modem to the e-book, a lot of software to navigate the connectivity, and an interface to walk Ernie through the process.

And so on. *The point is, even a single target-customer profile starts off a chain of issues that any product manager serious about developing a particular market opportunity must pursue to a satisfactory conclusion.*

Now, in the case of an electronic book, you might imagine a fairly lengthy list of potential target customers and target applications. In addition to maintenance repair people like Ernie, one could imagine:

- Doctors doing diagnoses or writing drug prescriptions (in which case it should be a lot smaller, support Boolean search arguments, and be able to display special symbols).
- Lawyers, doctors, real estate agents, and others seeking to pass a certification exam (in which case it should support simple quizzing).
- College students with heavy reading loads (in which case it should be supported by all the major publishers, be downloadable over a 56KB modem, and incorporate an intellectual property management system that allows for excerpts and partial royalties).
- General readers in remote locations such as surveyors or field scientists (in which case, in addition to the connectivity, it should support an e-commerce system for browsing and buying books).
- Outdoor readers (in which case it should have special lighting or screen characteristics to compensate for glare).

As even this cursory listing indicates, *every additional new target customer will put additional new demands on the whole product.* That is, the total sum of products and services needed in order to get the desired benefit changes any time you change the value proposition. It soon becomes clear to even the most optimistic product marketing managers that they cannot go after all markets at once, that at minimum they have to sequence and prioritize opportunities, and that each opportunity has very real support costs.

Now, given the need for a whole product in order to fulfill the customer's reason to buy, what is the responsibility of the tablet computer hardware vendor—and specifically of the product marketing manager who has the tablet PC as his product—for seeing that this whole product is in fact delivered? The answer is, it has nothing to do with responsibility, it has to do with marketing success. If you leave your customer's success to chance, you are giving up control over your own success. Conversely, by thinking through your customer's problems—and solutions—in their entirety, you can define—and work to ensure that the customer gets—the whole product.

At no time is this marketing proposition more true than when crossing the chasm. Prior to the chasm there is some hope that the visionaries will backfill the whole product through their own systems integration efforts. Once the product is established in the mainstream, there is some hope that some third party will see an opportunity for itself to make money fleshing out the whole product. *But while you are crossing the chasm, there is no hope of any external support that is not specifically recruited by you for this purpose.*

Some Real-World Examples

To see how this works out in actual practice, let's turn now to some specific industry examples. Basically, there are two types of scenarios we want to work through—one where there is installed competition, and the other where there is not. In the former case, it is as if one is trying to invade Normandy from England, and the installed market leader is playing the role of the Nazi forces. In the latter, it is as if one had landed on a new continent and decided to set up shop selling wares to the natives. Neither task is for the faint of heart.

Lawson Software and Client-Server Business Applications

To begin with the competitive example, imagine yourself back in 1993 as a $40 million business applications software company, located in Minneapolis, Minnesota, early to make the move to client-server architecture, and therefore currently included in the list of market leaders. The market has not crossed the chasm. Instead, the media is picking up on the first burst of enthusiasm for client-server applications. Your companions on the media hotlist are PeopleSoft and Oracle, both already out in front of you. Oracle, in particular, is more than an order of magnitude bigger than you, and PeopleSoft is the media darling. You have never even heard of know about SAP—the eventual dominant leader in this market which is probably just as well as then you really would have been sick to your stomach. The point is, if this were a car race, they have Grand Prix racing staffs and you and your brother are entered in your street car. *Now what?*

Oddly enough, Lawson decided that it *had the advantage* (this is a form of optimism that can only be built in the Midwest—it has something to do with the winters). It knew that to be interesting and viable as a company going forward, it had to become a market leader in something. Its advantage was that it *knew* it couldn't be the overall market leader, and that it had to focus immediately, if only to survive. Commitment to focus is the critical success factor for crossing the chasm, something very hard to gain in larger institutions which are always looking for big market returns right out of the box. Lawson was pretty sure that it could get a multi-year head start in a niche market by focusing right at the start, and that's precisely what it did.

There were several areas where the company had market momentum that could be developed into niche leadership, the two most prominent of which were health care and retail. It chose to focus on health care for two key reasons. First, with the advent of capitated health insurance that came early in the 1990s, the finance function in healthcare was thrown into turmoil, with all of its existing computer systems needing dramatic overhaul in order to provide critical information on costs. Second, the health care segment was consolidating into a relatively small number of major customers. This made it more attractive because it meant that a smaller company could dominate the segment sooner. When segments are too large or diffuse, early leaders can be displaced by fast-following competitors who have greater resources to apply to the opportunity.

As the campaign got under way, even this focus needed to be sharpened, and the target narrowed to a beachhead segment called integrated delivery networks or IDNs, entities formed by the merger of clinics, hospitals, and physician practice groups. This was an emerging segment, so it was not on the radar screens of the traditional marketing teams—hence it was easier for Lawson to steal a march on its larger competitors. Within it the target customer was the CFO and staff, and the compelling reason to buy was the desperate need to get pricing control over a new business model, to be able to understand revenue and costs by patient, by procedure, by fixed asset, by healthcare plan, and the like—because that was how the rest of the world proposed to pay them going forward.

Now the definition of the whole product is the minimum set of products and services needed to fulfill the compelling reason to buy for the target customer. In that light, Lawson built the following offer:

- *Core application software,* running on top of Unix hardware, to fulfill the standard needs of any financial organization, including a general ledger, accounts receivable, accounts payable, fixed assets, and the like. This was the price of entry. (Note: at the time customers had no interest in support for NT nor for the Internet—these were added subsequently, the latter with particularly dramatic impact.)
- An integrated *activity-based costing module* designed for maximum flexibility that allowed the organization to analyze and then capture costs and revenues by patient, by procedure, or by any other variable in the business mix. This was a godsend because it operated outboard of the core financial system and thus users could execute what-if scenarios with great freedom.
- *Materials management software* to minimize waste and increase return on both high-volume inventories of low-cost items (intravenous fluids, needles), and low volume-inventories of very high-cost items (artificial hips, interocular lenses, and the like). This required some healthcare-specific development, including supporting a unit of inventory management called the PAR cart, something akin to a delivery truck that travels the halls of the hospital replenishing its various rooms. No other client-server financials vendor supported PAR carts at the time, so Lawson was able to use this one feature as a signal of its special level of commitment to the segment.
- *Internet integration* which allowed IDNs to rapidly deploy new business processes on a common and consistent basis.

This "digital nervous system" became a critical prerequisite for capturing returns from the economies of scale that IDNs deliberately seek to achieve.

- *Workflow software* to ensure that as IDNs reengineered their business processes to improve their cost-effectiveness, the new procedures could be woven into the financial and materials management systems without major disruption. This came along with training not just in the software but in workflow analysis and the construction of new procedures.

- *Interfaces to legacy applications systems,* particularly those in patient management. The two market-leading vendors in this area are SMS and HBOC, neither of which chose to make Lawson their strategic partner (too small). So Lawson had to go the extra mile to make sure these interfaces worked effectively. (Later on the company's market leadership approach would have its reward, with SMS terminating a relationship it had with PeopleSoft and installing Lawson as its strategic partner, based on the company's success in penetrating the IDN market.)

- Finally, healthcare finance organizations simply needed *support,* somewhat in the sense of therapy. Every vendor offered the standard training and installation package, but Lawson went the extra mile and lined up consultants who could advise and train on active-based cost accounting, help set up and tune the system to get the kind of answers the CEO was demanding, and in some cases, help go get the answers ahead of the system in a crisis. These relationships were the most valued of all, and Lawson's role as a trusted advisor helping to bring the interested parties together, further exemplified its commitment to the niche.

What was the result of all this focus on a single niche? Early on, the results were underwhelming. In the first year of the program, Lawson's healthcare revenues doubled, but they still were less than 10% of total revenues. Review showed that the sales force was too thinly spread, and so the company reorganized to support a dedicated healthcare unit. In the next year revenues increased to 15% and the following to more than 20%. By mid-1998's close of fiscal year, healthcare was more than 30% of revenues, and the company had grown in five years from $40 million to $200 million. Most importantly, despite a fast-follower attack by PeopleSoft, Lawson has emerged as the acknowledged market leader in healthcare.

The game is not over, of course. SAP and Oracle have declared healthcare to be strategic, and PeopleSoft has not folded its tent. But Lawson successfully achieved a position of strength, in a game where from the outset it was surrounded by larger, better known, and better financed competitors. Moreover, it is expanding outward from its initial beachhead, both into other healthcare organizations, and taking into other service-related businesses seeking to use scale and process management to meet cost pressures, notably retail franchises in fast food. Whole product elements built for healthcare turn up to have surprising applicability in these new areas, and Lawson's future is targeted on a niche by niche market growth plan.

Savi and the Real-Time Inventory Tracking Market

Now let's turn to the other scenario for crossing the chasm, the one where (good news) there is no enemy fortifying the shore against invasion because (bad news) nobody thinks there is anything there to defend. Here the vendor must create a market out of whole cloth. Here the pragmatist buyers who are the key to the mainstream market do not reject the new product so much as simply watch it for signs of development. They don't say no, in other words; they just don't say yes. Talk about extended sales cycles!

In this situation, entrepreneurs are fighting a race against time. Like the intrepid explorers and colonists of the 16th and 17th centuries, they have landed in terra incognita and have a fixed amount of supplies (working capital) to see them through to self-sufficiency. The question is not whether someday someone will make a successful colony; the question is whether it will be them, or whether they will die in the attempt.

Let's look at a specific example. In 1992 a small start-up in Mountain View won a major contract from the Pentagon for an inventory tracking system. The system was based on radio-frequency tags attached to inventory containers interacting with a radio-frequency interrogation device that could poll the tags for their location and associated contents. It turned out that in Desert Storm, although the military was able to get record amounts of inventory to the battle zone in record time, it then could not easily find any specific inventory item once it was on site. This meant lots of opening up of containers to find out what was inside—fun at Christmas, perhaps, but not under combat conditions. Savi's devices allowed military logistics managers to conduct these same searches automatically, and during the next deployment, in the Bosnian theater, they came through with flying colors. Good show, and all that. *Now what?*

To cross the chasm based on a military product commits one to a procurement system that does not lend itself to superior financial returns, to a marketing system that is completely divorced from commercial markets, and to a whole lot of very long, not very stimulating meetings. It is virtually impossible to keep the attention and commitment of a bright R&D team in Silicon Valley with such a prospect, and so the management of Savi began to cast about for a commercial beachhead for crossing the chasm. Fortunately, it was ready to hand, for the commercial marketplace has the equivalent of such battle zones in every shipping yard in the world.

It's the same challenge. You know the inventory is here somewhere, but where is it exactly? If it is perishable inventory, you would like to find it before you smell it. If it is non-perishable, you would like to find it and get it to the right place in the right manufacturing line before the line has to stop for lack of inventory. As the world moves to Just-In-Time inventory management, this latter need goes from being nice to have, to being mission-critical. Savi did an early project with the Toyota Corporation which taught it hugely valuable lessons in Just-in-Time management disciplines, and it decided to make the extension of that project the basis for its beachhead attack.

In this market, the target customer is the yard manager, and the compelling reason to buy is to sustain a just-in-time inventory flow that is mission-critical to the enterprise's approach to operations. Recalling that the whole product is the minimum set of products and services needed to fulfill the compelling reason to buy for the target customer, Savi built the following whole product plan:

Savi Products

- *Gatemaster,* a tractor/trailer detection and identification system that detects, collects, monitors and reports on tag information obtained from tags attached to fleet tractors and/or trailers entering a dedicated yard area.
- *Yardmaster,* a wireless communications system linking hostlers (the people who work in the yard) with dispatch functions, thereby automating trailer movement assignments and improving workforce utilization.
- *Dockmaster,* a real time system that makes trailers arriving at dock doors immediately visible to the software applications governing shipping and receiving operations.
- *Passive RFID Tags* for each truck or tractor trailer to carry identification and contents information.
- *RFDC Handheld Terminals* for both vehicles and hostlers to interrogate tags and upload information into other systems.
- *Asset Manager,* a middleware software architecture, to take uploaded information from the yard and dock systems and integrate it with existing back-office systems.

Savi Services

- *Site Surveys and System Integration.* Due to the complexity of each installation, some level of system integration is always required. However over time, Savi will seek to convert as much of this function into "tool kits" to allow most typical integration requirements to be handled on-site by third parties.
- *Alarms and Custom User Interface Software.* Currently, as part of each installation there is significant customization of the system to handle specific alarms and other user-interface related development. Initially this is provided as a professional service offer. Again however, over time and as feasible, the company will seek to kit up these capabilities to offer more options deliverable at lower cost.

Non-Savi Products and Services

In any whole product, there are typically elements that the sponsoring company either cannot or should not provide. This is where partners and allies come in. In the case of Savi, this includes the following:

- *Wintel PC-based Server*, to keep costs down and conform to market standards.
- *Inventory management systems*, which could come from a wide variety of vendors, focused on shipping and receiving, manufacturing scheduling, supply chain planning, or the like.
- *Business process reengineering consulting* to help management teams redesign their processes, business relationships, communications procedures, and metrics, to ensure they can meet the challenges of Just-in-Time operations.
- *Training*, especially in the new processes and behaviors. At the outset of the market, Savi will train on its own systems itself, but over time it will seek to delegate that task to third-party partners.
- *Sales and service*, once the market is well under way, to be turned over to value-added resellers.

School is still out on the final outcomes of the Savi effort. In the midst of this effort the company, a wholly owned subsidiary of Raytheon, was in play. But the offer itself has been taken up by enough additional customers to ensure the company's ongoing place in the market—and that is the primary goal for crossing the chasm.

In the case of both Lawson and Savi, a commitment to the whole product led to an extended shopping list of products and services. Not all of these fell inside the core competence of the companies. Thus whole product marketing sent them in quest of partners and allies.

Partners and Allies

Marketing partnerships and strategic alliances are very trendy items in high-tech marketing these days. One expects to see ads in the *Wall Street Journal* any day now reading:

> Large, well-heeled company with established distribution channels and aging product line seeks small, entrepreneurial,

cash-starved technology leader with hot new product. Photos available upon request. Write box no. . . .

As a rule, however, these types of alliances do better in the boardroom than on the street. To start with, the company cultures are normally too antithetical to cooperate with each other. Decision cycles are wildly out of sync with each other, leading to enormous frustration among the entrepreneurs and patronizing responses from the established management. To make matters worse, each side has probably misrepresented itself one way or another during negotiations, such that there is plenty of ammunition for each group to fire at the other once tempers get hot. This is particularly likely to be the case when the entrepreneurs have been using acquisition as essentially a financial exit strategy. So, for the most part, despite the impeccable logic of these mergers, they are very tough to bring off.

Of course, some strategic alliances have been extremely successful. Consider the relationship that developed among SAP, Hewlett-Packard, and Andersen Consulting to displace IBM as the premier enterprise vendor by bringing client-server ERP (Enterprise Resource Planning) systems to market. Or consider the alliance between Intel and Microsoft, what some have called the Wintel duopoly, which to this day orchestrates the PC industry. Both these alliances have been hugely powerful and moved mountains of market cap. Powerful as these relationships are, however, the complexities of developing and maintaining such strategic alliances are enough to daunt all but the most megalomaniacal. They are certainly not the province of mere product managers seeking to ensure that their customers achieve their compelling reasons to buy.

What does work for product managers, on the other hand, are tactical alliances. *Tactical alliances have one and only one purpose: to accelerate the formation of whole product infrastructure within a specific target market segment.* The basic commitment is to codevelop a whole product and market it jointly. This benefits the product manager by ensuring customer satisfaction. It benefits the partner by providing expanded distribution into a hitherto untapped source of sales opportunities.

In this context, one need look no further than the Internet to see such emerging alliances at work. First it began with one between Netscape and Yahoo!, where the former sent traffic to the latter, so the latter could help people find valuable or enjoyable sites, and thus create more demand for the former's product. And as Yahoo! became a portal site—a stepping off place for entering the Internet—it became an alliance partner with commerce sites like Amazon.com and E*Trade deflecting traffic to their sites. Then, as companies like E*Trade sought to compete against established brands like Charles Schwab, they offered customers committing to their site free email service from vendors like Critical Path. And as other sites sought to attract and hold customers they bought advertising services from companies like U.S. Interactive or Link Exchange and marketing services from companies like Post and CKM. All of this, of course, created more business for the tools companies like Microsoft and Symantec, catalog companies like Aspect and ReQuisite, server companies like Compaq and Sun, service companies like Viant and Scient and a legion of others, all intertwining to bring Internet commerce into existence. The Internet is the furthest thing in the world from a vertically integrated market. It simply would not work without the web of alliances.

These types of alliances can often be readily initiated and managed at the product marketing manager level. Typically, the initial opportunity is first brought to the company's attention either by the salespeople or by customer support staff, one of whom has bumped into the potential ally at a particular customer's site. But they can also be anticipated through the exercise of thinking through the whole product solution to the customer's buying objective. The main point, again, is that these are tactical alliances growing out of whole product needs, not strategic alliances growing out of . . . well, whatever strategic alliances grow out of (my personal feeling is that the number-one cause of strategic alliances is too many staff people with not enough to do).

To see how this might work out in a single case, consider the case of Pharsight Corporation, a software start-up focused on the pharmaceuticals industry. It set itself the task of creating a whole new category, *Computer Assisted Trial Design*. The target customer is the executive in charge of drug trials. The compelling reason to buy is that as many as half of current drug clinical trials—which are hugely expensive and take painfully long to complete—deliver inconclusive results. Better trial design is the answer to this problem, but to date that has been more the province either of advanced statisticians (special science) or experienced clinicians (black art), and not a discipline accessible to mere mortals.

Pharsight has brought to market software to structure trial design in systematic repeatable ways and to draw on the learnings of prior trials to build models of how future trials might turn out. The market is still in its early phase, meaning that customers want to buy projects rather than products, and Pharsight has won market leadership through services-led offerings. This has led it to acquire the product lines of its primary competitors so that now, blending the three lines together, the company has a rich product offering. But that is not enough.

To model a trial one needs to have "model data"—that is, one has to input something to simulate outcomes based on past experience. Some of the models are reusable from trial to trial—patient population models which create benchmarks for how a control group might be expected to respond, for example, or design and analysis models for controlling for interactions among multiple variables. Other models will be specific to either a class of drug or a family of diseases. These latter often must be generated not from numbers or formally collected data but rather from capturing the opinion and experience of experts.

What makes all this so challenging is that pharmaceutical companies are intensely competitive with one another and do not want to share any knowledge which they think might be part of their competitive advantage. A lot of the models, in truth, should be, and no doubt eventually will be, in the public domain. That would make them accessible to companies like Pharsight who would add value to them through cataloguing, cross-referencing, and cross-verification. But none of this will help the Pharsight whole product manager in the short term, nor for that matter the company's customers. So how can one proceed?

Since the problem is just surfacing at the time of this writing, what follows is speculative but represents the range of thinking the company is exploring. One way forward is to explicitly partner with customers. Pharsight might well barter its own valued services in exchange for rights to productize and distribute certain portions of the data model. The customer would certainly want to protect the bits that would reveal its investigations, but with such incentives it might well share generic data that could be reused for common metrics. There really is no reason to reinvent the wheel on a population model, for example, since there is little competitive advantage in closely guarding one's own model and there would be great industry benefit in initiating and continuing to contribute to a robust multi-trial database. Partnering with customers will thus be a key component, the primary challenge not being technical, but rather cultural.

Another potential source of partnership are the public health agencies, who by contrast are highly motivated to pool and share learnings. In addition, however, they might be persuaded to take a more active role. Certain diseases like malaria, for example, are not attracting pharmaceutical investment simply for economic reasons. Death, however, is not an economist, which creates major problems for public health. If the public agencies were able to build data models into a common pool, this could reduce the investment to undertake certain types of drug research and attract more activity into the area without having to fund it directly.

A third source of model contributors could be the contract research organizations, the entities that actually conduct the scores of clinical trials needed to garner FDA approval. Productivity is their number one issue, and in return for productivity-enhancing software, they might well be persuaded to support building public data models, particularly if those same models could be reused in subsequent trials, thereby further increasing productivity.

A fourth approach—one taken by numerous companies in biotech—is to recruit an advisory board of scientists, typically from the university research community. These are the folks who actually run the clinical trials. Compensation is usually in the form of stock options, which provides financial leverage to the scientists, in return for which they contribute both work products and relationships. The latter can be extremely valuable in nudging a potential customer to make a contribution to a shared knowledgebase.

A fifth approach is to enlist the managed care organizations who can give data both from clinical trials and real-life medical practice. They would value the resulting models as a framework for their own practice guidelines, and in so doing would create another market opportunity where Pharsight could add value going forward.

Which of these partnership are most likely to succeed? While it's too soon to call, there is an encouraging underlying dynamic that Pharsight's whole product manager will be able to exploit. All these constituencies get together at conferences and trade shows all the time. This allows the company to explore multiple avenues in parallel cost-effectively. It also allows it to evangelize its ideas in forums where proactive constituencies from the public sector could help persuade colleagues in the private sector to buy in.

All in all this amounts to *creating a market*. For markets represent more than just a buyer and a seller. They are an ecology of interrelated interests interoperating to create what business schools call value chains. For any company crossing the chasm, fostering the initial partnerships to create the whole product is the equivalent of seeding the value chain, getting it started. Once value starts being generated, the market system becomes self-reinforcing, and the whole product manager's job then is simply to let go and get out of the way.

To sum up, whole product definition followed by a strong program of tactical alliances to speed the development of the whole product infrastructure is the essence of assembling an invasion force for crossing the chasm. The force itself is a function of actually delivering on the customer's compelling reason to buy in its entirety. That force is still rare in the high-tech marketplace, so rare that, despite the overall high-risk nature of the chasm period, *any company that executes a whole product strategy competently has a high probability of mainstream market success.*

Recap: Tips on Whole Product Management

Again, in keeping with our intent to recap key ideas at the close of each chapter through a tactical checklist, here are eight tips on whole product management:

1. Use the doughnut diagram to define—and then to communicate—the whole product. Shade in all the areas for which you intend your company to take primary responsibility. The remaining areas must be filled by partners or allies.
2. Review the whole product to ensure it has been reduced to

its mineral set. This is the KISS philosophy (Keep It Simple, Stupid). It is hard enough to manage a whole product without burdening it with unnecessary bells and whistles.

3. Review the whole product from each participant's point of view. Make sure each vendor wins, and that no vendor gets an unfair share of the pie. Inequities here, particularly when they favor you, will instantly defeat the whole product effort—companies are naturally suspicious of each other anyway, and given any encouragement, will interpret your entire scheme as a rip-off.

4. Develop the whole product relationships slowly, working from existing instances of cooperation toward a more formalized program. Do not try to institutionalize cooperation in advance of credible examples that everyone can benefit from it—not the least of whom should be the customers.

5. With large partners, try to work from the bottom up; with small ones, from the top down. The goal in either case is to work as close as possible to where decisions that affect the customer actually get made.

6. Once formalized relationships are in place, use them as openings for communication only. Do not count on them to drive cooperation. Partnerships ultimately work only when specific individuals from the different companies involved choose to trust each other.

7. If you are working with very large partners, focus your energy on establishing relationships at the district office level and watch out for wasting time and effort with large corporate staffs. Conversely, if you are working with small partners, be sensitive to their limited resources and do everything you can to leverage your company to work to their advantage.

8. Finally, do not be surprised to discover that the most difficult partner to manage is your own company. If the partnership really is equitable, you can count on someone inside your company insisting on taking a bigger share of the benefit pie. In fighting back, look to your customers to be your truest and most powerful allies.

6

Define the Battle

On the eve of our invasion, let us regroup. We have already established the point of attack, a target market segment plagued by a problem that gives them a truly compelling reason to buy. We have already mapped out the whole product needed to eliminate this problem and have recruited the necessary partners and allies to deliver it. The major obstacle in our way now is competition. To succeed in securing our beachhead we need to understand who or what the competition is, what their current relationship to our target customer consists of, and how we can best position ourselves to force them out of our target market segment.

This is what we mean by defining the battle. *The fundamental rule of engagement is that any force can defeat any other force—if it can define the battle.* If we get to set the turf, if we get to set the competitive criteria for winning, why would we ever lose? The answer, depressingly enough, is because we don't do it right. Sometimes it is because we misunderstand either our own strengths and weaknesses, or those of our competitors. More often, however, it is because we misinterpret what our target customers really want, or we are afraid to step up to the responsibility of making sure they get it.

How far most one go to serve one's customers? Well, in the case of crossing the chasm, one of the key things a pragmatist customer wants to see is strong competition. If you are fresh from developing a new value proposition with visionaries, that competition is not likely to exist—at least not in a form that a pragmatist would appreciate. What you have to do then is create it.

Creating the Competition

In the progression of the Technology Adoption Life Cycle, the nature of competition changes dramatically. The changes are so radical that, in a very real sense, one can say at more than one point in the cycle that one has no obvious competition. Unfortunately, where there is no competition, there is no market. By way of introduction, therefore, we need to rethink the significance of competition as it relates to crossing the chasm.

In our experience to date with developing an early market, competition has not come from competitive products so much as from alternative modes of operation. Resistance has been a function of inertia growing out of commitment to the status quo, fear of risk, or lack of a compelling reason to buy. Our goal in the early market has been to enlist visionary sponsors to help overcome this resistance. Their competition, in turn, has come from others within their own company, pragmatists who are vying with visionaries for dollars to fund projects. The pragmatists' competitive solution, in general, is to invest dollars to chip away at problems a piece at a time (whereas the visionaries aspire, like Alexander the Great with the Gordian knot, to cut through them with a single mighty—and mighty expensive—stroke). Pragmatists work to educate the company on the risks and costs involved. Visionaries counter with charismatic appeals to taking bold and decisive actions. The competition takes place at the level of corporate agenda, not at the level of competing products.

That's how competitions work in the early market. It is not at all how they work in the mainstream, in part because there are not enough visionaries to go around, in part because visionaries themselves like to play not in the mainstream but rather out in front of it. Now we are in the true domain of the pragmatist. *In the pragmatist's domain, competition is defined by comparative evaluations of products and vendors within a common category.*

These comparative evaluations confer on the buying process an air of rationality that is extremely reassuring to the pragmatist, the sort of thing that manifests itself in evaluation matrices of factors weighted and scored. And the conclusions drawn from these matrices will ultimately shape the dimensions and segmentation of the mainstream market. Windows PCs, it will turn out, are best for office automation, while Macintoshes still cling to some advantages for graphics. HP 9000's are best for manufacturing, Silicon Graphics workstations for film editing, and Sun SPARCstations for Internet servers. Pragmatist buyers do not like to buy until there is both established competition and an established leader, for that is a signal that the market has matured sufficiently to support a reasonable whole product infrastructure around an identified centerpiece.

In sum, the pragmatists are loath to buy until they can compare. *Competition, therefore, becomes a fundamental condition for purchase.* So, coming from the early market, where there are typically no perceived competing products, with the goal of penetrating the mainstream, you often have to go out and *create your competition.*

Creating the competition is the single most important marketing decision made in the battle to enter the mainstream. It begins with locating your product within a buying category that already has some established credibility with the pragmatist buyers. That category should be populated with other reasonable buying choices, ideally ones with which the pragmatists are already familiar. Within this universe, your goal is to position your product as the indisputably correct buying choice.

The great risk here is to rig the competition, that is, to create a universe that is too self-serving. You can succeed in creating a competitive set that you clearly dominate, but this set, unfortunately, is either not credible or not attractive to the pragmatist buyers. For example, I might claim that I am the greatest high-tech marketing consultant with a Ph.D. in Renaissance English literature. This claim might be credible, but it is not particularly attractive. On the other hand, I might claim that I am the greatest marketing consultant of all time—an attractive claim, perhaps (although it is not obvious to me how one can be a great consultant and egotistical at the same time) but, in any event, not a credible one.

In high-tech marketing, the sins may not be this egregious, but they are very widespread. I am familiar with products that claim to be leaders in such categories as "100% pure Java-enabled transaction processing servers," "CORBA-compliant, object-oriented messaging services," and "fault-tolerant Internet access gateways." These "categories" actually had meaning and value during the early market development for these products, because in each case a visionary could translate the technology component into an opportunity to make a strategic breakthrough. They are meaningless, however, to pragmatist buyers. Such categories neither relate to their concerns nor emerge from the world in which they work. Moreover, these categories appear specifically designed to exclude from the competitive set the very products the pragmatist is most likely to consider as purchase alternatives. As marketing devices for crossing the chasm, therefore, they are useless.

So, how can you avoid selecting a self-servicing or irrelevant competitive set? The key is to focus in on the values and concerns of the pragmatists, not the visionaries. It helps to start with the right conceptual model—in this case, *the Competitive-Positioning Compass.* That model is designed to create a value profile of target customers anywhere in the Technology Adoption Life Cycle, identify what to them would appear to be the most reasonable competitive set, develop comparative rankings within that set on the value attributes with the highest ranking in their profile, and then build our positioning strategy development around those comparative rankings. Here's how it works.

The Competitive-Positioning Compass

There are four domains of value in high-tech marketing: technology, product, market, and company. As products move through the Technology Adoption Life Cycle, the domain of greatest value to the customer changes. In the early market, where decisions are dominated by technology enthusiasts and visionaries, the key value domains are technology and product. In the mainstream, where decisions are dominated by pragmatists and conservatives, the key domains are market and company. Crossing the chasm, in this context, represents a transition from product-based to market-based values.

The Competitive-Positioning Compass illustrates these dynamics:

The Competitive-Positioning Compass

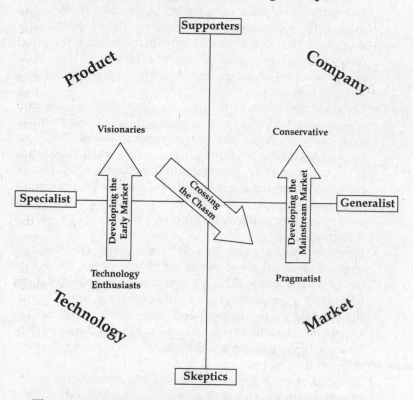

There is a lot of information packed into this model, so let's sort it out piece by piece.

- The directionality provided by the compass comes in the form of the two labeled axes. *The horizontal dimension shows the range of buyer interest in and understanding of high-technology issues.* In general, the early market is dominated by specialists who, by their nature, are more interested in technology and product issues than in market standing or company stature. By contrast, the mainstream is dominated by generalists who are more interested in market leadership and company stability than in the bits and bytes or speeds and feeds of particular products.

- *The vertical dimension overlays a second measure, the buyer's attitude toward the proposed value proposition, ranging from skepticism to support.* Markets begin in a state of skepticism and evolve to a state of support. In the case of the early market, the technology enthusiasts are the skeptical gate-keepers; in the case of the mainstream market, it is the pragmatists. Once they have given their blessings, then their companions—visionaries and conservatives, respectively—feel free to buy in.

- *The model also points to the fact that people who are supportive of your value proposition take an interest in your products and in your company. People who are skeptical of you do not.* This means that, at the beginning of a market, when skepticism is the common state, basing communications on product or company strengths is a mistake. You have no permission to tout these elements, because the market players do not yet believe you are going to be around long enough to make a difference.

- However, there are ways to win over skeptics. *Even the most skeptical specialists are always on the lookout for new technology breakthroughs.* Thus, although you cannot initially get them to sponsor your product, you can get them involved in understanding its technology, and from that understanding, to gain an appreciation for the product itself. The more they appreciate the technology, the easier it becomes for them to support the product.

- *Similarly, skeptical generalists may not take an interest in an unproven company but are always interested in new market developments.* If you can show the generalists that there is an emerging unmet market requirement, one that you have specifically positioned your products and your marketing efforts to meet, then out of their appreciation for the market opportunity, they can learn to appreciate your company.

- *These are the two "natural" marketing rhythms in high tech—developing the early market and developing the mainstream market.* You develop an early market by demonstrating a strong technology advantage and converting it to product credibility, and you develop a mainstream market by demonstrating a market leadership advantage and converting it to company credibility.

- *By contrast, the "chasm transition" represents an unnatural rhythm.* Crossing the chasm requires moving from an environment of support among the visionaries back into one of skepticism among the pragmatists. It means moving from the familiar ground of product-oriented issues to the unfamiliar ground of market-oriented ones, and from the familiar audience of like-minded specialists to the unfamiliar audience of essentially uninterested generalists.

Now let's tie all this back into creating the competition. If we are going to succeed in winning over the lower right quadrant, the skeptical pragmatists, then that competition has to be based in market-oriented concerns. That's what the pragmatists care about. In other words, we must shift our marketing focus from celebrating product-centric value attributes to market-centric ones. Here is a representative list of each:

Product-Centric	Market-Centric
Fastest product	Largest installed base
Easiest to use	Most third party supporters
Elegant architecture	De facto standard
Product price	Cost of ownership
Unique functionality	Quality of support

In the previous chapter, the entire basis of the focus on whole product and partners and allies was to move our leadership premise from the left-hand list to the right. That is, lacking an existing market leadership position, we wanted, within the confines of a manageable market segment, to create the valued attributes of one, and thereby bring a state of true market leadership into existence. Now we need to communicate what we have accomplished so as to win the pragmatist buyers' support.

To sum up, it is the market-centric value system—supplemented (but not superseded) by the product-centric one—that must be the basis for the value profile of the target customers when crossing the chasm.

This value profile, in turn, will model how the target customers are likely to perceive the competitive set and what position they are likely to accord to a new player coming into that set. Let's see how this works out in a real-world example.

Creating the Competition: The Example of Silicon Graphics

Creating the competition involves using two competitors as beacons so that the market can locate your company's unique value proposition. The first of these two competitors we will call the *market alternative*. This is a company that the target customer has been buying from for years. The problem they address is the one we will address, and the budget that is allocated to them represents the money we as a the new entrant are going to preempt. To earn the right to this budget, we are going to use a discontinuous product innovation to address a problematic limitation in the traditional offer.

The second reference competitor we will call the *product alternative*. This is a company that has also harnessed a discontinuous innovation—perhaps, but not necessarily, the same one we have—and is positioning itself like us as a technology leader. Their very existence gives credibility to the notion that now is the time to embrace a discontinuity. Our intent here is to acknowledge their technology but to differentiate from them by virtue of our own niche market focus.

Here's how it played out in the case of Silicon Graphics. The market they targeted was Hollywood, specifically the postproduction film editing process. Traditional editing was done by cutting and splicing film—literally—hence the phrase "the cutting room floor." But beyond a certain messiness, this method has a major limitation, namely, if the image you want didn't get on the film, there's not a lot you can do about it now, short of a hugely expensive reshoot.

Silicon Graphics was able to bring to this market a radically discontinuous innovation: If the image you want is not on the film, *put it there!* This is the magic of digital editing, its trump card over traditional analog methods. There is simply no way the traditional vendors could match it. As a result, they made perfect *market alternatives*. Referencing them made clear who was Silicon Graphics' target customer and what was the compelling reason to buy. It made clear what the whole product would have to be, what trade shows the company would have to go to, and what kind of people they would have to seek out as partners and allies.

At the same time, asking artists to embrace computers, and asking their producers to pay for them, creates a kind of credibility crisis. Just who is this Silicon Graphics and what exactly is a digital workstation. In order to shore up its credibility, the company needed a referenceable *product alternative*. Here both Sun and Hewlett-Packard fit in nicely. Both had Unix workstations that were leading edge and thus worthy product alternatives to Silicon Graphics. Both were famous companies. Both *validated* Silicon Graphics. At the same time, neither company had undertaken the exceptional commitments needed by the film industry. This could be demonstrated easily to a prospective customer simply by turning all three workstations around and looking at the ports coming out the back. Both Sun and HP had the standard ports for connecting to computer peripherals and networks. But the Silicon Graphics workstation, in addition to all these, had half a dozen other ports that hooked it to devices specific to the film-editing industry. It was obvious that they had made a niche commitment the others had not.

To sum up, your market alternative helps people identify your target customer (what you have in common) and your compelling reason to buy (where you differentiate). Similarly, your product alternative helps people appreciate your technology leverage (what you have in common) and your niche commitment (where you differentiate). Thus you create the two beacons that triangulate to teach the market your positioning.

A Second Example: Quicken

In the case of Silicon Graphics, there was a preexisting market of film editors who were saddled with a broken mission-critical business process. This is the ideal market condition for a beach-head landing. But not everyone gets dealt so nice a hand. Consider the plight of any innovative consumer product, for example. It is usually able to capture the attention of the technology enthusiasts, but once that class of customers is exhausted, or rather falls prey to attention deficit disorder and wanders off to look at the next "cool tool," what is the vendor to do? There are no visionaries in consumer markets to underwrite major ongoing R&D. Nor are there typically mission-critical processes to fix. Now what? Let's look at how a company called Intuit tackled this problem with a product called Quicken.

Quicken, from a PC specialist's point of view, belongs to a category of software called financial management applications for home use. Today it is the market leader. There was a time, however, when the success of the product—and the company—hung by a thread. How Intuit, and its president Scott Cook, responded to that situation provides a superb lesson in how creating the right competition can accelerate crossing the chasm.

When Quicken was first introduced into the market, the best-selling program was Andrew Tobias's *Managing Your Money*. From a product-centric point of view, it was far richer in functionality than Quicken, offering portfolio analysis and other financial modeling capabilities. To the "financial enthusiasts" who made up the early market for these products, it was clearly the preferred choice, and Intuit was doomed if it continued to play the game on that turf.

In casting about for alternatives, Intuit hit on very simple value proposition for the home computer user—make it easier to pay bills. This is a pragmatist type of value proposition—we are not making a strategic breakthrough but rather an incremental improvement in a recurrent operation. It is, in other words, a marketing opportunity for the mainstream, not the early market.

Unfortunately for Intuit, there was no established mainstream category called computer-aided bill paying. Pragmatists used checkbooks, thank you very much, and they worked just fine. So how could Intuit penetrate this market?

First, they had to find a manageable market segment. In this case, the world was already pretty well restricted by the qualifier, adults who use computers in their home. The key issue then became checks—if Quicken were to be easier than a manual system, it had to be easy to get the checks. Intuit decided to handle that process for their end user. (As a result, today, income from providing checks is a key component of the company's business strategy, the margins being excellent and the cost of sales virtually nil.) Then a third issue arose—how to align the checks with the printer correctly so that everything printed in the right spot. This turned out to be a major technical problem, ultimately requiring Intuit to invent a subsequently patented solution. Once that was accomplished, however, a true whole product was in place.

Now we come to *creating the competition.* Can you see how it falls out? The market alternative is paper and pen checking. That is the familiar alternative. What we are going to offer is more speed and convenience during bill paying *plus* the opportunity to control one's finances by seeing where the money goes *plus* a much more organized set of resources with which to tackle tax time. Please note these are not really broken processes so much as sort of bent processes—hence the slipperiness of the slope that Quicken had to climb to get out of the chasm. But they were compelling, particularly to PC owners looking for more ways to leverage the technology at home. Thus if you were a home PC user and a bill payer, you knew that Intuit wanted you.

The product alternative was Managing Your Money. Rather than fight it in a features war, Intuit could now use it as a reference beacon. *That* product, they could say, is the one for financial enthusiasts who want to analyze their investment portfolios. *This* product is for ordinary householders paying their monthly bills. How can you tell? Well, look at how simple we have made it to use. Look at our checkbook interface metaphor. Look at the way we handle the checks themselves.

To close on this example, this is what we mean by defining the battle. You choose your competition to help you define the niche market you will dominate. As long as they are well behaved and stay out of your niche, you go out of your way to honor their achievements elsewhere. If they should stray into your niche, on the other hand, you must defeat them totally. The beachhead segment must be your niche and yours alone, separated from all others by tall barriers to entry. Just remember your Robert Frost— "Good fences make good neighbors."

Creating the Competition:
Some Current Opportunities

So much for looking backward. Hindsight is always 20/20. Let's see what happens when we try to create some competition for products that are just now crossing the chasm.

Three worth looking at are Channelpoint, Diffusion, and VerticalNet. All three at the time of this writing are "pre-chasm" with early adopter customers, and all are contemplating their chasm-crossing strategies. None of them is anything like a household name. This presents a major positioning challenge. Now we know that the one place an unknown company is welcome to position itself is in an "empty space," fulfilling an unmet need. The problem is that no one wants to listen very long to hear about it. Here is where using two familiar reference beacons as the market alternative and the product alternative comes in so handy.

Channelpoint: Reengineering the Insurance
Distribution Chain

Channelpoint of Colorado Springs represents the intersection of a group of Internet-savvy engineers that spun out of Sun with a visionary management team that saw in the traditional insurance distribution system a process crying out to be reengineered. Today in health insurance, for example, there is a chain that begins on the supply end with 1) underwriting insurers, who develop products which are then communicated to 2) general agents, who aggregate offerings from many insurers and present them to 3) independent agents, who present an appropriate subset to 4) potential clients who, with the independent agent's help, select the best offering, which leads back to 3) the independent agent writing up an application (each company's being a little different) and seeking clarifications from 2) the general agent who either knows or has to go back to 1) the underwriting insurer to get the answer. As we often like to say about early software products, this system may be hard to use but at least it's slow.

Channelpoint intends to use the Internet to reengineer this process. It will initially team with or acquire general agents who have aggregated content and convert that content to Internet format. It will simultaneously migrate a portion of the support desk from telephone to the Internet as well, with email as the initial communication channel, moving to chat and IP telephony as needed. At the same time, it will work with the independent agents in the relationship to get them Internet ready at their end—it only requires a browser and a willing attitude. Later on in the process, the company will help extend the Internet back into the insurer's domain to facilitate their application processing workflow, but just bridging the general and the independent agent domains can take a huge chunk out of the cost and delay in the system. Later still one can envision the end customer also getting involved, initially to inquire about claims or premiums, eventually to submit either or both.

All in all, it is a very interesting business idea, so how to position it? The market alternative is clearly the traditional general agent. By mentioning this category and calling out two or three of the better known firms, Channelpoint can immediately capture the attention of their target market—and simultaneously let the rest of us tune out. This last consequence is not only good for us but good for Channelpoint, as they do not want to clog up their sales and marketing communications channels with irrelevant inquiries.

OK, now that we have called out the industry's most stalwart firms, how in the world can a no-name start-up hope to compete credibly? Here is where we invoke our product alternative. This should be a well-known example of a technology-based offer that reengineered the way a mature industry brokered its value-chain relationships. One of the most visible of these is the SABRE System which reengineered the way that the airlines distribute tickets. Channelpoint positions itself, in other words, at the intersection of 1) the general agent for property and casualty insurance with 2) the SABRE System for brokering community interactions. It uses its SABRE-like technology to differentiate from the traditional general agent, and it uses its niche insurance industry focus to differentiate from a SABRE-like Internet competitor such as Yahoo!. In a bar, when asked what Channelpoint does, I can now say, "Oh, they're the SABRE System for the insurance industry."

Now, it is not that I am encouraging you to hang out in bars, or even to suggest that I do very often myself (although I am peculiarly susceptible to a fine Cabernet). Rather the point is that the level of attention one anticipates in a bar is about on par with what a no-name start-up can expect, on first acquaintance, from a potential customer, partner, or investor. And so it is crucial that it be able to cut through the noise with a curt phrase that can register even upon the most unattentive neurons.

Diffusion: Communications for Customer Retention

At the time of this writing, Diffusion is a start-up in Silicon Valley focused on leveraging the explosion in electronic communications channels—Internet, fax, email, office phone, pager, cell phone, PDA—to help companies such as banks and brokerages provide increasingly more customer-delighting interactions with their most valued clientele. Their essential offer has three dimensions.

1. To their customers' clients, it is a promise to communicate with them via whatever channel they themselves prefer. Thus I might ask to be emailed most information but to be paged with urgent items, whereas Marie might prefer print catalogs or a phone call, and Michael might want to get a fax.

2. To the customers themselves, the offer is to improve customer management by cross-connecting all the various touchpoints in their customer contact system. Thus, today my bank might have several programs contacting me— direct mail, a personal web page, a phone call from an account manager—all operating as independent silos. Diffusion's technology integrates all these mechanisms into a single system for customer relationship management.

3. In addition to the proliferation of outbound media reflected above there is a parallel internal proliferation of content sources, be they customer information systems for taking and confirming orders or providing customer service or support, marketing systems such as catalogs or direct mail, or publishing systems both from internal web sites and via dynamic extraction from front-office databases. Thus a marketing group seeking to provide a differentiated relationship with valued clients has a daunting set

of tasks facing it if the system is to scale to any size. Again, enter Diffusion with a technology to map all the "gozintas" to all the "gozoutas."

Now one of the challenges that a start-up like Diffusion faces is that customers have no budget set aside for purchasing the new offer because they didn't even know the *category* existed, much less the company or the product. Here again choosing the right *market alternative* is key. Basically, you are choosing the budget upon which you intend to poach.

In the case of Diffusion, one path would be to target "Gold Club" account management budgets as the market alternative. These budgets are under the control of Diffusion's target customer, and they address the key benefit—clientele retention—that Diffusion seeks to enhance. The problem today is that Gold Club programs are too expensive to use for any but the bank or brokerage's most valued clients. But by focusing here, Diffusion can give prospective customers the mental positioning experience of, "Oh, so you are a way I can extend my customer relationship management programs more cost-effectively?" That gives them a place to park the company, in terms of budget and authority to make the buying decision.

Now comes time for the *product alternative*. Here Diffusion faces a special challenge. There is no direct product alternative that matches up well to what they do. There is a *project alternative*—that is, an early market offer—to accomplish the same goals, building out a custom system with a technology vendor like Broadvision or an enterprise systems partner like IBM. The problem with choosing an early market offer as the competition is that pragmatist customers want to see something comparable already across the chasm before they buy in. So what is Diffusion to do?

One path is to choose an *analogous product* as the product alternative. This is not a buying choice but it does provide a point of reference for appreciating the usefulness and practicality of the new offer. In the case of Diffusion, one possible analogous offer is the customer profile systems that airlines and travel agencies provide. While they do not specify information flow, they do build a customer profile for repeat clients that captures their travel preferences to ensure better service automatically. By analogy, Diffusion's position might be, "Oh, so you're a customer profile system for managing our account relationships with Gold Club clients."

Now this is not a perfect fit by any means, but it is within range. High-value customer management is the market, and customer profiling is a key product attribute, albeit not the only one. At minimum it is better than starting with, "We're an Internet-enabled, multi-media outbound communications facility for one-to-one marketing programs based on client-provided communication channel preferences" or some other such mind-numbing concatenation of abstractions that, when said to your mother, makes her eyes cloud over with worry for her misdirected offspring.

VerticalNet: Internet Sites for Microsegments

VerticalNet, at the time of this writing (I keep using this phrase because, with the arrival of Internet time, God knows what will be operative in the world by the time you are reading this paragraph), is a start-up focused on creating destination sites for highly specialized vertical markets, most of which have an engineering spin to them. The good news is, the competition is not stiff. Where else in the world, for example, could you find an entire website called *www.solidwaste.com*? But if you are an environmental engineer looking for specialized industry information, this thing is a gold mine. Click on the Buyer's Guide and a veritable cornucopia of offers unfolds. Say you are attracted to *sludge collection*. Click there, and wait, there's more! Fifteen or so subtopics emerge. Heart aflutter, you click on *Removal (wastewater sludge)*, and then, *mirabile dictu*, not one, not two, but *twenty* different companies are listed, all of which offer this service, one in the area near you!

But say it was a slow day. Then instead of searching in Yellow Pages fashion, you could content yourself with browsing the industry news, entering a chat group on your favorite solid waste topic, or sitting on a live interview with a solid waste guru (possibly an oxymoron). Could Dilbert ever be made happier? Honestly, this is what the Internet was made for. VerticalNet just has to get the word out.

The question is, to whom? Who is the customer? It turns out

if you are a media play, then your customer is either an advertiser or a vendor selling on your site. It is not Dilbert with whom you need to position but rather the people who want to sell to him. And since the world of solid waste is not under any market pressure to reengineer itself, you can expect that it is filled with conservatives, not visionaries, and that Internet advertising expenditures or Internet reseller commission programs are *not* in their current budget. Now what?

Choosing the competition is key here, and VerticalNet has moved wisely. As its market alternative, it identifies the leading trade magazine that services whatever target market it is going after. Indeed, in some cases it has gone so far as to recruit the editor of that magazine to join its team. The site then becomes an interactive forum based on the same news, same issues, and *same advertisers,* as the trade magazine. It is a true *"zine."* This makes it very easy for conservative buyers to identify the dollars they would use to experiment with this new medium.

As its product alternative, VerticalNet points to Internet community sites like America OnLine. Even conservatives have heard of this company, and its success in creating virtual communities communicates exactly the phenomenon that VerticalNet wants to highlight in its own positioning. "Oh, you're sort of an AOL for specialized vertical niches." Yes!

In Closing

Let met just close this section with a heads-up alert. If you try out this exercise of choosing the competition, and have trouble finding a single, clear market alternative, this is a clue. It means that you are not ready to cross the chasm. Chasm-crossing requires a single target beachhead segment, and in that segment, there needs to exist already the budget dollars to buy your offer. To be sure, the budget will be "misnamed," because it will be allocated to some brain-dead, ineffective Band-Aid approach to solving what has become a broken, mission-critical process. But it must exist, or else you will lose a full year just in educating the market to put aside money that might be used to buy your product in the following year.

Choosing your market alternative wisely is the solution to this problem. But it has to be credible. And understand that, as soon as you call out your choice, you are in for a fight. That market alternative, whoever it may be, had plans for that money. Indeed, it considers that budget as *its budget*, and it will not take kindly to your actions.

That's where the product alternative comes in. You need to make clear to everyone involved that a technology shift is under way here, and that old solutions simply cannot hope to keep up. Trade magazines on their best day cannot be interactive. Direct mail programs on their best day cannot catch me at the golf course. General agents on their best day cannot provide round-the-clock answers to independent agents' questions—at least not cost-effectively. It is not your intent to deride the performance of the established Old Guard. Indeed, you should honor it, as your target customer has long-standing relationships with these vendors. Rather, it is to suggest that a new wave is coming, and that you intend to domesticate that technology to the same ends as these tried-and-true solution providers.

So, market alternatives call out the budget and thus the market category, and product alternatives call out the differentiation. It sounds a lot like positioning, the topic to which we will now turn.

Positioning

Creating the competition, more than anything else, represents a watershed moment in positioning. Positioning is the most discussed and least well understood component of high-tech marketing. You can keep yourself from making most positioning gaffes if you will simply remember the following principles:

1. *Positioning, first and foremost, is a noun, not a verb.* That is, it is best understood as an attribute associated with a company or a product, and not as the marketing contortions that people go through to set up that association.

2. *Positioning is the single largest influence on the buying decision.* It serves as a kind of buyers' shorthand, shaping not only their final choice but even the way they evaluate alternatives leading up to that choice. In other words, evaluations

are often simply rationalizations of preestablished positioning.

3. *Positioning exists in people's heads, not in your words.* If you want to talk intelligently about positioning, you must frame a position in words that are likely to actually exist in other people's heads, and not in words that come straight out of hot advertising copy.

4. *People are highly conservative about entertaining changes in positioning.* This is just another way of saying that people do not like you messing with the stuff that is inside their heads. In general, the most effective positioning strategies are the ones that demand the least amount of change.

Given all of the above, it is then possible to talk about *positioning* as a verb—a set of activities designed to bring about *positioning* as a noun. Here there is one fundamental key to success: When most people think of positioning in this way, they are thinking about how to make their products *easier to sell.* But the correct goal is to make them *easier to buy.*

Companies focus on making products easier to sell because that is what they are worried about—selling. They load their marketing communications with every possible selling argument, following the age-old axiom that if you throw a lot of mud at a wall, some of it is bound to stick. Prospective customers shrink from this barrage, which in turn causes the salespeople to chase after them that much harder. Even though the words appear to address the customers' values and needs, the communication is really focused on the seller's attempt to manipulate them, a fact that is transparently obvious to the potential consumer. It's a complete turn-off—all because the company was trying to make its product easy to sell instead of easy to buy.

Think about it. Most people resist selling but enjoy buying. By focusing on making a product easy to buy, you are focusing on what the customers really want. In turn, they will sense this and reward you with their purchases. Thus, easy to buy becomes easy to sell. The goal of positioning, therefore, is to create a space inside the target customer's head called "best buy for this type of situation" and to attain sole, undisputed occupancy of that space. Only then, when the green light is on, and there is no remaining competing alternative, is a product easy to buy.

Now, the nature of that best-buy space is a function of who is the target customer. Indeed, this space builds and expands cumulatively as the product passes through the Technology Adoption Life Cycle. There are four fundamental stages in this process, corresponding to the four primary psychographic types, as follows:

1. *Name it and frame it.* Potential customers cannot buy what they cannot name, nor can they seek out the product unless they know what category to look under. *This is the minimum amount of positioning needed to make the product easy to buy for a technology enthusiast.*

Discontinuous innovations are often difficult to name and frame. The largely ineffectual category *middleware* is an attempt to name and frame a new class of systems software that lives between established platforms of enabling technology—the operating system, the database, and the network operating system—and established applications— say, financials, human resources, or sales force automation. It turns out that businesses are wanting to make all these applications interoperate, and to do that requires messaging software, transaction processing software, object brokering software, and the like. It is all very complicated technically and gives rise to sectarian fanaticism which nobody wants to deal with, so as an industry we have collectively agreed to throw it all in a bucket called middleware, and hope we can just keep a lid on it. The problem with all this is that we cannot keep it in the bucket. The need for it keeps calling it out. But once it gets out, because we cannot name it and frame it properly, all companies who provide it are stuck with a nasty marketing problem. Customers go into prolonged review cycles, religious wars break out, and sales get postponed as each situation battles over the same tired ground.

Recently there has been something of a breakthrough in this space with the rise of a category called *enterprise application integration* or EAI. This phrase displaces *middleware,* a word which does nothing more than reference a location in a software systems hierarchy, with a phrase that communicates a critical benefit. It also *frames* the space by confining it to applications integration, and even more specifically, by the word enterprise, to high-end server applications. There is a clear market alternative here—all the money companies pay systems integrators to do this work—and so the market should now be able to move on.

2. *Who for and what for.* Customers will not buy something until they know who is going to use it and for what purpose. *This is the minimum extension to positioning needed to make the product easy to buy for the visionary.*

This is the challenge for the electronic book. It has been named and framed quite well, but it is not clear who is going to buy it or for what reason. It is the same sort of challenge that smartcards face in the United States. As it becomes clear who can most benefit from these technologies to achieve a major strategic advantage, then they will have secured the necessary positions to develop their respective early markets.

3. *Competition and differentiation.* Customers cannot know what to expect or what to pay for a product until they can place it in some sort of comparative context. *This is the minimum extension to positioning needed to make a product easy to buy for a programatist.*

Examples of this category have filled the preceding pages of this chapter. The key is to provide the reassurance of a competitive set, and of a market-leading choice within that set.

4. *Financials and Futures.* Customers cannot be completely secure in buying a product until they know it comes from a vendor with staying power who will continue to invest in this product category. *This is the final extension of positioning needed to make a product easy to buy for a conservative.*

Microsoft, IBM, Oracle, and Intel are all long-standing blue-chip companies with whom conservatives feel comfortable. Emerging blue-chips like SAP and Cisco also create this comfort factor, and so can smaller companies if they can dominate a niche market, the way Documentum has done in pharmaceuticals, and Lawson Software in health care.

The purpose of positioning is to put in place these sets of perceptions with the appropriate target customers in the appropriate sequence and at the appropriate time in the development of a product's market.

The Positioning Process

When positioning is thought of primarily as a verb, it refers to a communications process made up of four key components:

1. *The claim.* The key here is to reduce the fundamental position statement—a claim of undisputable market leadership within a given target market segment—to a two-sentence format outlined later in this chapter.
2. *The evidence.* The claim to undisputed leadership is meaningless if it can, in fact, be disputed. The key here is to develop sufficient evidence as to make any such disputation unreasonable.
3. *Communications.* Armed with claim and evidence, the goal here is to identify and address the right audiences in the right sequence with the right versions of the message.
4. *Feedback and adjustment.* Just as football coaches have to make half-time adjustments to their game plans, so do marketers, once the positioning has been exposed to the competition. Competitors can be expected to poke holes in the initial effort, and these need to be patched up or otherwise responded to.

This last component makes positioning a dynamic process rather than a one-time event. As such, it means marketers revisit the same audiences many times over during the life of a product. Establishing relationships of trust, therefore, rather than wowing them on a one-time basis, is key to any ongoing success.

The Claim: Passing the Elevator Test

Of the four components, by far the hardest to get right is the claim. It is not that we lack for ideas, usually, but rather that we cannot express them in any reasonable span of time. Hence the elevator test. Can you explain your product in the time it takes to ride up in an elevator? Venture capitalists use this all the time as a test of investment potential. If you cannot pass the test, they don't invest. Here's why.

1. *Whatever your claim is, it cannot be transmitted by word of mouth.* In this medium the unit of thought is at most a sentence or two. Beyond that, people cannot hold it in their heads. Since we have already established that word of mouth is fundamental to success in high-tech marketing, you must lose.

2. *Your marketing communications will be all over the map.* Every time someone writes a brochure, a presentation, or an ad, they will pick up the claim from some different corner and come up with yet another version of the positioning. Regardless of how good this version is, it will not reinforce the previous versions, and the marketplace will not get comfortable that it knows your position. A product with an uncertain position is very difficult to buy.

3. *Your R&D will be all over the map.* Again, since there are so many different dimensions to your positioning, engineering and product marketing can pick any number of different routes forward that may or may not add up to a real market advantage. You will have no clear winning proposition but many strong losing ones.

4. *You won't be able to recruit partners and allies,* because they won't be sure enough about your goals to make any meaningful commitments. What they will say instead, both to each other and to the rest of the industry, is, "Great technology—too bad they can't market."

5. *You are not likely to get financing from anybody with experience.* As just noted, most savvy investors know that if you can't pass the elevator test, among other things, you do not have a clear—that is, investable—marketing strategy.

So how can we guarantee passing the elevator test? The key is to define your position based on the target segment you intend to dominate and the value proposition you intend to dominate it with. Within this context, you then set forth your competition and the unique differentiation that belongs to you and that you expect to drive the buying decision your way.

Here is a proven formula for getting all this down into two

short sentences. Try it out on your own company and one of its key products. Just fill in the blanks:

- **For** (target customers—beachhead segment only)
- **Who are dissatisfied with** (the current *market alternative*)
- **Our product is a** (new product category)
- **That provides** (key problem-solving capability).
- **Unlike** (the *product alternative*),
- **We have assembled** (key whole product features for your specific application).

Let's try this out with a few examples, starting with some we have already looked at earlier in the chapter.

Silicon Graphics in Hollywood

- For post-production film engineers
- Who are dissatisfied with the limitations of traditional film editors
- Our workstation is a digital film editor
- That lets you modify film images any way you choose.
- Unlike workstations from Sun, HP, or IBM,
- We have assembled all the interfaces needed for post-production film editing.

Intuit

- For the bill-paying member of the family who also uses a home PC
- Who is tired of filling out the same old checks month after month
- Quicken is a PC home finance program
- That automatically creates and tracks all your check-writing.
- Unlike *Managing Your Money*, a financial analysis package,
- Our system is optimized specifically for home bill-paying.

Now what is often interesting about writing a statement like this is not what you write down but what you have to give up. In the case of Silicon Graphics, the workstation can be used with all kinds of programs besides film editing per se—film editors could run project management software on it, access the Internet, send email, keep databases of customer contacts, and the like. And in the case of Intuit, Quicken also lets you budget more effectively, and it keeps records for tax season that can be fed directly into Intuit's Turbo Tax for home filing. Wouldn't it have been better to load in these extra value statements for a bigger effect?

The answer here is an emphatic *no!* Indeed, this is just what defeats most positioning efforts. *Remember, the goal of positioning is to create and occupy a space inside the target customers' head.* Now, as we already noted, people are very conservative about what they let you do inside their head. One of the things they do not like is for you to take up too much space. This means they will use a kind of shorthand reference: Mercedes ("top-of-the-line, conservative"), BMW ("upscale performance sedan, yuppie"), Cadillac ("American top-of-the-line, tired"), Lexus ("New kid on the block, current best buy"). That's all the space you get for your primary differentiation statement. It's like a telegram with less than one line. If you don't make the choice to fill the space with a single attribute, then the market will do it for you. And since the market includes your competition trying to unposition you, don't count on it to be kind.

Let's try another example, this one from one of our start-ups:

Channelpoint

- For insurance providers distributing through independent agents
- Who can no longer afford to bear the overhead of the general agent system
- Channelpoint is an Internet-based insurance distribution system
- That uses computers to provide round-the-clock service to selling agents.
- Unlike Yahoo!, or any other general-purpose Internet services site,
- We provide the complete suite of information and services needed to support your field selling force.

Note how the two reference competitors, the market alternative and the product alternative, help the listener's mind triangulate to find the new position. Positioning is not about hype. It is about clear and precise direction.

One final point on claims before moving on to other issues: *The statement of position is not the tag line for the ad.* Ad agencies come up with tag lines, not marketing groups. The function of the statement of position is to control the ad campaign, to ensure that however "creative" it may become, it stays on strategy. If the point of the ad is not identical with the point of the claim, then it is the ad, not the claim, that must be changed—regardless of how great the ad is.

The Shifting Burden of Proof

The toughest thing about high-tech marketing is that just about the time you get the hang of something, it becomes obsolete. This is even true of something as innocent as providing evidence. That is, like everything else in high tech, the kind of evidence that is needed evolves over the course of the Technology Adoption Life Cycle. This can be summarized within the structure of the Competitive-Positioning Compass:

By working your way up the left and then up the right of the compass, you can trace the evolution of desired evidence as the market evolves from the technology enthusiast to the visionary to the pragmatist and conservative. The key point to notice is the transition from product to market, corresponding to crossing the chasm. This is simply a corroboration of a point we have been making all along, that pragmatists are more interested in the market's response to a product than in the product itself.

What is particularly awkward for a high-tech company making this transition is that for the first time the major sources of desired evidence are not directly under its control. This is not a matter of having the right features or winning the right benchmark war. It is a matter of other people—theoretically disinterested third parties—voting to endorse your product through not only words but deeds. It is actual investment in building the whole product that demonstrates to the pragmatist that if you are not already the market segment leader, you are destined to become so.

In sum, to the pragmatist buyer, the most powerful evidence of leadership and likelihood of competitive victory is market share. In the absence of definitive numbers here, pragmatists will look to the quality and number of partners and allies you have assembled in your camp,

Positioning: The Evidence

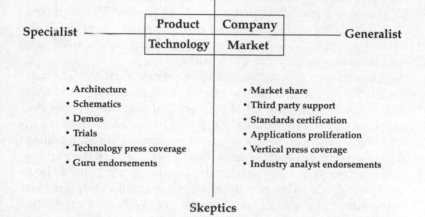

Supporters

Specialist · · · · · · · · · Generalist

Product	Company
Technology	Market

* Benchmarks
* Product Reviews
* Design wins
* Initial sales volumes
* Trade press coverage
* Visionary endorsements

* Revenues and profits
* Strategic partners
* Top tier customers
* Full product line
* Business press coverage
* Financial analyst endorsements

* Architecture
* Schematics
* Demos
* Trials
* Technology press coverage
* Guru endorsements

* Market share
* Third party support
* Standards certification
* Applications proliferation
* Vertical press coverage
* Industry analyst endorsements

Skeptics

and their degree of demonstrable commitment to your cause. The kind of evidence this buyer is looking for is signs of comarketing, such as joint sales calls and cross-referencing each other's products in sales literature, and consistent mutual support even when the other party is not present in the room.

This point leads directly into communications strategy for crossing the chasm. Not only do you have to develop this kind of evidence of whole product support; you also have to make sure that everyone hears about it.

Whole Product Launches

The concept of a *whole product launch* is a derivative of the widely known practice of a product launch. That is, whenever a new

high-tech product is introduced, it is customary to launch it by
first briefing the industry analysts and long-lead press editors
well in advance of the launch date (so they can serve as references), and then taking the top company executives on a tour to
the weekly trade press the week prior to announcement, with the
announcement itself capped by an event.

These product launches work just fine when the product itself
is "new news." Then, they are an appropriate tool for the development of early markets. By the same token, however, they are
not appropriate for crossing the chasm. At this point the product
is not new news—at least it had better not be if we are planning to
win over the pragmatist buyer. The trade press is not interested,
therefore, in a great trumpeting article on Release 3.0 (not unless,
that is, you are a Microsoft, but that's another story). So if the
message is not "Look at my hot new product," then what is it,
and how are you going to get it out?

The message now is "Look at this hot new market." The message typically consists of a description of the emerging new market, fed by an emerging set of partners and allies, each supplying
a part of the whole product puzzle, to the satisfaction of an increasingly visible and growing set of customers. The lure embedded in this story is that we are seeing a new trend in the making,
and everyone who has a seat on this bandwagon is going to be in
on The Big Win. This is a great story for small entrepreneurial
companies to be able to tell, because it gives them a credibility
that they cannot achieve on their own. Their product does not
even have to be at the center of the puzzle—it just has to be an
indispensable piece, as Oracle's relational database is to ERP regardless of which application vendor is chosen, or Rambus's
memory interface will be in upcoming generations of PCs, regardless of which PC vendor is chosen.

Now, how can marketing communications improve your
odds? First, marketers have to pick the right communications
venue. There are two venues, in general, that lend themselves to
whole product stories. The first is the business press. Whole
product stories, particularly ones sparked by partnerships and
alliances coming together to bring off some wonderful result for
a particular company, are the bread and butter of business fare.
Companies organizing to bring off this feat consistently, and
thereby dominate a particular market segment, are particularly

of interest. If the company is brand new, to be sure, the business press is leery. In this instance it is important first to build some references in the financial analyst community, based not on the company per se but on the market opportunity it has in its sights. Financial analysts are usually quite open to briefings on emerging market opportunities, and in that context, can be wooed to take an interest in an emerging entrepreneurial venture. Once they have bought into the market, then they can be used as a reference point by the business press in developing a story.

In bringing this story to the business press, it is important to bring along as many of the other players in the market as possible. One effective tactic is to hold a press conference with multiple spokespersons on the dais—customers, analysts, partners, distributors, and so on. A more elaborate version of the same approach is to sponsor a conference on the core issue that is driving the development of this market. The key objective in either case is to communicate the bandwagon effect in progress.

Finally, communicating via the business press has to be done within the framework of a big idea. Technology stories, told at the level of technology, are only interesting as vignettes, squibs for the column that leads the second section of the *Wall Street Journal*. For a technology story to be a *business story*, it has to be about something that transcends high tech. Typically, the seed of the story is either a new type of opportunity or problem that can now be addressed effectively because of advances in the industry. These advances will have been sparked by technology breakthroughs, and that will be part of the story, but they are now seen to extend to the entire whole product infrastructure, and that will be the main thrust of the story.

The great benefit of the business press as a medium of communication is its high degree of credibility across virtually all business buying situations. This is a two-edged sword for the entrepreneurial company. In order to preserve its credibility, the business press is reluctant to endorse entrepreneurial enterprises until they have been well proved. It takes a long time, in other words, to earn coverage. On the other hand, having broken through in this medium once, it is much easier to do so again. Furthermore, subsequent product-oriented coverage in the trade press tends to become more thorough as the company attains greater stature in the business press.

So building relationships with business press editors, initially around a whole product story, is a key tactic in crossing the chasm. In addition to the business pres, the other communications channel for getting out a whole product message is what could be loosely termed "vertical media"—that is, media specifically dedicated to a particular industry or a particular profession. Industry trade shows and conferences, meetings of professional associations, and publications dedicated to a specific market segment all tend to attract pragmatists and conservatives, people who put a high value on maintaining relationships within their group. These associations are relatively open to participation from supporting vendors, provided that the vendors are not too obtrusive with their sales messages.

Whole product issues are ideal for this kind of communications. The idea is to get in a room with a number of people in a given industry and outline the current state of affairs in the vendor's marketplace as it relates to their business. Correctly framed, these sessions put the customer, rather than the vendor or the vendor's product, at the center of things. They align themselves with the customer's needs and the alternatives available to meet those needs. Thus, although they are at one level clearly self-serving to the vendor, they do not *feel* self-serving, positioning the vendor more as a consultant than as a salesperson.

The goal of a whole product launch campaign, overall, is to develop relationships in support of a positive word-of-mouth campaign for your company and products. The first thing to remember is that developing these relationships takes time—time to ferret out who are the key influencers, time to get to know them on more or less equal footing, time to get up to speed on the industry issues so that the relationship is pertinent and valuable to both parties. The other thing to remember is that, once these relationships are in place, they represent a major barrier to entry for any competitor. Pragmatists and conservatives—the core of any mainstream market—like to do business with people they know.

Recap: The Competitive-Positioning Checklist

To define the battle effectively so that you win the business of a pragmatist buyer, you must:

1. Focus the competition within the market segment established by your must-have value proposition—that is, that combination of target customer, product offering, and compelling reason to buy that establishes your primary reason for being.
2. Create the competition around what, for a pragmatist buyer, represents a reasonable and reasonably comprehensive set of alternative ways of achieving this value proposition. Do not tamper with this set by artificially excluding a reasonable competitor—nothing is more likely to alienate your pragmatist buyer.
3. Focus your communications by reducing your fundamental competitive claim to a two-sentence formula and then managing every piece of company communication to ensure that it always stays within the bounds set out by that formula. In particular, always be sure to reinforce the second sentence of this claim, the one that identifies your primary competition and how you are differentiated from it.
4. Demonstrate the validity of your competitive claim through the quality of your whole product solution and the quality of your partners and allies, so that the pragmatist buyer will conclude you are, or must shortly become, the indisputable leader of this competitive set.

7

Launch the Invasion

In this chapter the final pieces of the D-Day strategy come into play—distribution and pricing. As we launch our invasion across the chasm, distribution is the vehicle that will carry us on our mission, and pricing is its fuel. These two issues are the only two points where marketing decisions come into direct contact with the new mainstream customer. Decisions in both distribution and pricing, therefore, have enormous strategic impact, and, with distribution in particular, there is typically only one chance to get it right. For this reason, we have put these two last in our invasion planning sequence, so that we could have the advantage of nailing everything else down first.

The number-one corporate objective, when crossing the chasm, is to secure a channel into the mainstream market with which the pragmatist customer will be comfortable. This objective comes before revenues, before profits, before press, even before customer satisfaction. All these other factors can be fixed later—but only if the channel is established. Or, to put it the other way around, if the channel is not established, nothing further can be accomplished. Finally, given that establishing the channel is the number-one goal, the fundamental function of pricing during this same period is to achieve this same end. In other words, during the chasm period, the number-one concern of pricing is not to satisfy the customer or to satisfy the investors, but to *motivate the channel*.

To sum up, when crossing the chasm, we are looking to attract *customer-oriented distribution*, and one of our primary lures will be *distribution-oriented pricing*. These are somewhat radical words, and they are going to require considerable discussion. In order for this discussion to make any sense, however, we need first to review the somewhat tumultuous state of distribution as we are poised to enter the next century. There is, at present, a structural problem in the distribution function for high tech, one that may well work itself out eventually, but probably not in time to solve any of our immediate problems. Once we understand that problem, then we can better chart our chasm-crossing strategy.

The Structure of High-Tech Distribution

There are currently a wide variety of distribution channels operating under the umbrella of the high-tech market. The most prominent are the following:

- *Direct sales*. Typically national in scope and focused on calling on major accounts, this consists of a dedicated sales force in the direct employ of the vendor, with no other intermediary between the customer and the company. IBM has the most famous direct sales force in the world.
- *Two-tier retail*. In the retail market, this represents a distributor like Merisel, Techdata, or Ingram playing the first-tier role, which is backward-facing toward the supply chain, and an outlet such as Compuware playing the customer-facing role. Vendors ship to the first tier which stages inventory and manages credit for the second tier. This structure, which was at its most powerful during the late 1980s, is increasingly being displaced by the next two channels.
- *One-tier retail*. These are the superstores, like CompUSA and Fry's, that for the bulk of goods sold fulfill both the wholesale and retail functions in a single entity. Increasingly squeezed profit margins are forcing this restructuring,

especially in the PC market where so much of the product line has been commoditized.

- *Internet retail.* This is either one or two tier and is optimized for consumer offers that do not need significant configuration or support. (The fact that Dell does both is a testimony not to the channel but to the company—witness the difficulty its competitors had matching up.)

- *Two-tier value-added reselling.* For products that are too complex for retail, the two-tier model continues to work when the customer-facing role is played by a VAR. These are typically "no-name" companies which specialize in a particular technology (say, websites) or a particular vertical market, (say, CAD or publishing), and operate normally within the confines of a single city.

- *National roll-ups.* From time to time the market makes a move to "roll up" local VARs into a nation-wide chain. The first attempts were tried with the Netware VAR network during the 1980s but fell afoul of Novell's fall from grace. More recently, U.S. Web is attempting a similar strategy with Web VARs. Most successful to date, perhaps, has been ICON with its roll-up of copier sales and service outlets upon which it is now seeking to overlay PC, LAN, and Web service provisioning.

- *OEMs (Original Equipment Manufacturers).* This is at least a two-tier transaction, beginning with a direct sales force selling to manufacturers, who then integrate the purchased product into their own systems, and sell the systems on to the customer. If the OEM product is bought through industrial distributors and sold through retail or VARs, there can actually be as many as four tiers to this channel. The big computer manufacturers, just like the big auto makers, all purchase products on an OEM basis from the rest of the industry.

- *Systems integrators.* This is not a channel per se, since it rarely if ever sells the same products twice. Rather it is a project-oriented institution for managing very large or very complex computer projects. Since, however, such projects often "design in" standards that are then replicated throughout the rest of the company's operations, there are good reasons to treat systems integrators like a channel.

But all of the above to some extent shrinks in comparison to the looming impact of the greatest change to distribution methods perhaps ever—namely, the Internet. The challenge this poses for chasm-crossers facing the turn of the century is that most of this impact has yet to be felt, and planning on the Internet channel for the short term is not a good strategy. Just as important, however, is the opposite caveat: Not planning for the Internet as part of your long-term distribution strategy will be fatal. The cost of interacting on the Internet with either a prospect or a repeat customer is so much lower, and the ability to shape that experience is so much higher, that every commercial enterprise will have to incorporate this medium eventually.

Channels are optimized for different purposes, as follows:

1. *Demand creators versus demand fulfillers.* Direct sales forces, for example, are optimized for creating demand, while retail superstores are optimized for fulfilling it. A lot of other channels commit to do both, are optimized for neither, and suffer the consequences.

   When crossing the chasm, our immediate goal is to create mainstream demand, but we must also look ahead toward putting in place a channel that can fulfill it.

2. *Role in providing the whole product.* Systems integrators and VARs are optimized for playing a very large role in providing or developing the whole product, and make much of their profits from this service. By contrast, retail and Internet channels take a low-cost position, based on the assumption that the whole product is already "institutionalized" and can be fully assembled from off-the-shelf parts. Again, there are a number of channels caught in the middle, the most visible of which at the moment is the mall-based retail storefront.

   In the chasm case, the goal is to take the burden of whole product off of the channel in order to free it up to spend more time creating—and fulfilling—demand for the product.

3. *Potential for high volume.* In some ways, this is simply the obverse of the previous category. Channels optimized for whole product development are not effective for high volume delivery. There is too much labor in their business

mix, so that when business is booming, they tend to slow down their selling efforts to work off some of the backlog— thereby flattening what could otherwise be meteoric growth. The low-cost, low-service channels are just the opposite. Optimized for high volumes, they are great for boom times, but they do not do well in start-up mode and tend to panic and dump when business softens, thereby trashing not only their own margins but yours as well.

In the chasm case, our ultimate target is likely to be a high-volume channel. This is something like getting a car into high gear. The question is, How do we get it up to speed?

What we are looking for, in general, as we cross the chasm, is the following: First and foremost, does the channel already have, or is it optimized to create, a relationship with our target mainstream customer? If not, then it is not a candidate for helping us cross the chasm. If, nonetheless, it is our customer's ultimate preferred form of distribution, then we are going to have to look for a two-step process, where we have an intermediate distribution tactic to create the relationship and a longer-term one to reap maximum rewards.

Second, how will this channel fit into our whole product mix—our partners and allies strategy? The less pressure we put on the channel to deliver the whole product, the more it can focus on selling instead of supporting. On the other hand, it is absolutely critical that our mainstream customer gets the whole product, and we should be willing to sacrifice some volume in order to prevent customer dissatisfaction at getting less than the whole product.

With these factors in mind, let's take a closer look at some of the more prominent channels in operation today, and specifically, how they stack up against our immediate goal of crossing the chasm.

Direct Sales

Historically, the most consistently successful channel in high tech has been the direct sales force. More than anything else, it was

IBM's mastery of this medium that drove it to prominence, and then dominance, in the 1960s and 1970s. Other companies have successfully copied this act, be they DEC and HP for mid-range systems, Oracle and Computer Associates for systems software, SAP and PeopleSoft for enterprise application software, or Cisco and Ascend for networking hardware.

The direct sales force is optimized for creating demand. At its center is a consultative salesperson who works with the client in needs analysis and then, supported by a team of application and technology specialists, develops and proposes solutions, which, after additional interaction with the customer, and a competitive procurement, turn into purchase orders. This is a very expensive way to sell, with the cost of sales built into the product's price. It works reasonably well when two conditions are met.

For the customer, the key condition is that the vendor supply a broadly comprehensive and reasonably competitive set of offerings. If this condition is not met, it means that additional vendor interactions are needed. There is only so much time and effort the customer is willing to put into educating and negotiating with vendors, so breadth of product line is crucial here.

For the vendor, the key condition is both the volume and the predictability of revenues. To support a single consultative salesperson requires a revenue stream of anywhere from $500,000 to several million dollars, depending on the amount of presales and postsales support provided. Say our quota is $1,200,000. That means we must close $100,000 per month. If the sales cycle is six to nine months, and if we are able to close one out of every two opportunities, then we have to have either 12 to 18 $100,000 prospects in the pipeline at all times (not very probable) or some smaller number of significantly larger deals going.

One underlying point here is that there is a price point below which this method of distribution cannot work. If we have to be working $500,000 opportunities, we cannot be selling a product whose base price is $20,000. It turns out the practical limit for base-product price point is around $75,000, with variations depending on the level of selling support required and the speed and predictability of the sales cycle.

Another underlying point is the importance of what salespeople call *account control* but which might more accurately be termed *account cooperation*. Direct sales forces can bring lots of service to an account, but not if they lose the deal during the competitive procurement. Basically then, for this system to work, there has to be a fundamentally *uncompetitive* agenda operating, a you-scratch-my-back-and-I'll-scratch-yours agreement under which vendors are granted a limited monopoly, subject to their not exploiting it egregiously and continuing to provide premium service. This confers a high degree of predictability of revenue and a lower cost of sales.

When functioning at its best, within the limits just laid out, direct sales is the optimal channel for high tech. It is also the best channel for crossing the chasm. Nonetheless, it is currently under heavy fire from a number of different directions.

First, wherever vendors have been able to achieve lock-in with customers through proprietary technology, there has been the temptation to exploit the relationship through unfairly expensive maintenance agreements topped by charging for some new releases as if they were new products. This was one of the main forces behind the open systems rebellion that undermined so many vendors' account control—which, in turn, decrease predictability of revenues, putting the system further in jeopardy.

A second consequence of the open systems competition has been the dramatic increase in the relative value or "price/performance" of computers, and the consequent drop in average selling price. This has been further exacerbated by the rise of NT, displacing the Unix servers at the low end and beginning to move upstream, further commoditizing the platform and driving out the opportunity to preserve product margins through proprietary differentiation. As price points lower, it becomes increasingly difficult to sell through a direct sales force. This, in turn, puts heavy pressure on companies with direct sales forces already in place—the minicomputer companies in the Northeast are a prime example—to field sufficient product to generate the kind of revenue volumes needed to maintain this high overhead channel.

Working against the success of that effort is the fact that the complexity of total solutions has increased to the point where no single vendor can cover a big piece of the pie. This undermines the primary customer benefit of account cooperation with a direct sales force—the simplifying of vendor relationships and the improved accountability of working with a single vendor. Now there are too many cooks involved, and major accounts are looking to other kinds of channels—notably, systems integrators—for this kind of overall problem simplification.

Now, against this background, let us look at direct sales as a distribution alternative for crossing the chasm. To qualify at all, our product must have an appropriate pricepoint, so let's assume it does. We like a direct sales approach because it is optimized for creating demand, something very much on our minds. What then are the issues to consider?

Our first issue is, Can we get our sales force entry into the pragmatist's restricted domain? Obviously, if you hire good enough people and hammer loud enough at the door, you can gain some level of entry. What we really mean here is, Do we have a partner or ally who already has a relationship with our target customer and who can help open the door from the inside? Without that sort of leverage, a direct sales force, particularly in its first year of existence, can be very expensive indeed, as you can end up paying very high wages to people who are essentially spending most of their time doing low grade prospecting—and resenting every minute of it.

A strong tactic to consider here is hiring a senior executive out of the target community to become your company's ambassador back in. This should be someone who has a deep understanding of the business issues in the community and relationships of longstanding that can be leveraged to introduce sales teams to appropriate prospects. The alternative to this is to rely on a strategic partner's relationships, but this is dangerous because you need direct access to the entire customer organization if you are going to emerge from this market as its leader. Nonetheless, it can be done, and this approach will be discussed later in this chapter under "Selling Partnerships."

Our second issue is, Do we have the capability to recruit and grow a direct sales force appropriate to the market opportunity? It is certainly possible for a company to create outstanding early market success and not have any significant kind of sales force management capability. Indeed, such capabilities may be countercultural to the firm. If such is the case, then setting out to build a direct sales force can be a very dangerous proposition. An all too typical failed scenario begins with bringing in one or more high-priced, highly ambitious sales executives, who, in trying to create a winning sales situation, run roughshod over the existing culture, politicize the management environment, create divisiveness both within the executive staff and between that group and its investors, and, in general, reduce the effectiveness of the team just at the time when it is being most challenged.

A reasonable alternative here is to field a direct sales force as a transition-oriented tactic, with a long-term goal to take the product into a different channel, through a selling partnership. This will represent a major reduction in overall return on investment—since he who owns the customer owns the profit margins and the future of the product—but it also represents a major reduction in risk, and potential grief. This is not the macho high-tech way, of course, which in my view gives it added attractiveness.

All other things being equal, however, direct sales is the preferred alternative because it gives us maximum control over our own destiny. And as we also noted, even if we cannot pass these tests, because creating demand is so important when crossing the chasm, we may well want to copy many techniques from direct sales to supplement, or transition to, whatever distribution channel we finally select.

Retail Sales

The second most successful channel in high tech has been the retail sales organization brought into existence by the personal computer and its ever-broadening, highly institutionalized whole product entourage. That is, what the PC brought to the industry for the first time was an open platform with standard hardware and software interfaces. This meant that thousands of vendors could create and supply the parts of an industry-standard whole product, thereby institutionalizing that whole product and opening up the opportunity for retail.

Since its initial appearance in the 1980s with stores like The Byte Shop, retail sales has continually evolved and morphed along with the PC industry. There was a time, for example, when dedicated stores looked like the right venue, and both IBM and Xerox experimented with same. But it soon became clear the selection rather than brand was the driving force, with an additional emphasis on service to the business customer. At this stage

Businessland and Computerland rose to prominence. Then, as the PC became increasingly commoditized, larger and larger storefronts gained competitive advantage, and we saw the rise of superstores like CompUSA and Fry's. Concurrently, catalog stores like PC and Mac Warehouse created a mail-order channel. Then for a while the big consumer warehouse outlets like The Price Club and Wal-Mart had the inside track, particularly for the home market, while on the business side, new challengers emerged in Staples and Office Depot. Most recently direct distribution as practiced by Dell Computer has become the most effective channel, whether customers are interacting over the phone, or increasingly now, over the Internet. Overall, retail offers a staggering array of alternatives, and if we are going to be successful in crossing the chasm, we need to step back and operate from the first principles.

First and foremost, the retail system works optimally when its job is to fulfill demand rather than to create it. Unlike direct sales, it does not support the consultative sale. It cannot explain complex software or facilitate complex integration of products. It is not, in other words, well set up to be a participant in developing the whole product. Rather, it is structured to leverage an institutionalized whole product by supporting convenient access to a broad selection of brand choices, providing these choices at the lowest possible prices, and, in the process of so doing, serving as a credit broker among the intermediary parties in the distribution chain.

Now, in a sense, as far as crossing the chasm is concerned, we need go no further. *Because it does not create demand, and because it does not help develop whole products, retail distribution is structurally unsuited to solving the chasm problem.* The overwhelming bulk of retail sales go to companies that have solidly established brands—that has always been the bias of retail whether the shelves are filled with hardware or software or with clothing or consumer package goods. If you need to create demand, you need much more focus and face time than the traditional outlet can provide. Dedicated outlets in retail—think Starbucks, the Body Shop, or Smith & Hawkins—can help drive new brands into the market, particularly if they are backed up by catalog sales, but to date the only comparable outlet that has emerged in high tech has been around the cell phone. For the most part, retail simply cannot sponsor discontinuous innovations because they require the channel to spend a disproportionate, and ultimately unproductive, amount of time on something that gives too low a rate of return.

The ultimate consequence of this for the retail channel is extremely serious. In a typical supermarket, more than a thousand new products are introduced in a single year, and much of the volume sold through comes from these promotions. To be fair, these products are not really "new"—most are simple repackagings or a minor variation on an already accepted good—but they do have at least some novelty to offer. High-tech products, by contrast, tend to be "really new"—as in incompatible with the prior release and the various comarketed products that accompanied that release. To introduce this kind of novelty requires coordinating a host of collateral products and staffing a sales force that understands what goes with what. It is a ruinous modification to the retail formula, and until the industry truly matures, it puts all such channels in a deep quandary.

So let us rephrase our interest in the retail channel. Let's say we have a product that—*once it is established in the mainstream market*—will be a natural candidate for retail distribution. Now, how should we proceed?

Simply put, we need some intermediary step during which we can create the demand and institutionalize the whole product, and then turn it over to the channel. Some proven approaches include the following:

1. *Direct response advertising.* This works particularly well for developing demand for low-priced software products, such as Intuit's Quicken, the check-writing package for use in the home or small business, where the risk of trial is not great and the whole product infrastructure is already in place. By varying the pitch in the ads, marketers can sort out which reasons to buy are truly compelling. Once the demand itself is demonstrated, and the pitch proven, then the product can be readily absorbed by the channel.

2. *Telesales (and teleservice).* This works better for higher priced products, like Dell's line of PC-compatible computers, where the company was able to target a particular kind of pragmatist customer—power users—and provide them with better-than-retail service through highly trained and

motivated people working over the phone. The low cost of sales was passed on to these customers as lower prices, and because the customers were unusually knowledgeable, even complex product discussions could be accomplished without face-to-face meetings and demos. And now that Dell's brand has been established "voice to voice," it is branching out over the Internet to create even lower cost of sales as customers engage in the first generation of self-service purchasing of high-tech products.

3. *Value-added resellers.* Later we are going to discuss this channel separately, analyzing its suitability for long-term participation in the mainstream market, but here we are looking at it simply as a transitional vehicle. It is an excellent vehicle for developing whole product support, although it is not particularly motivated to package or institutionalize these solutions. It is only fair at creating demand, for, although it uses a consultative approach, it tends to be dominated by problem solvers rather than salespeople, and so sometimes lacks basic selling skills. Nonetheless for whole products which simply cannot commoditize easily, ones that have some level of irreducible complexity, the VAR channel can often be the right choice for crossing the chasm. We saw this in the 1980s where Novell succeeded with LANs and Autodesk with PC CAD, and we are seeing it in the 1990s where Internet VARs are setting up the first generation of websites for small businesses.

All three of these techniques, then, serve the chasm-crossing strategy by bridging between an immediate need to create demand and/or institutionalize the whole product, after which the product can be turned over to the retail channel in order to leverage that channel's high-volume capabilities.

Now because this product will ultimately end up in retail, there's an upper limit to its price point, typically a few thousand dollars for a consumer up to perhaps $10,000 for a small business owner. Beyond that point, demands for service and other elements of the whole product simply exceed the retail channel's ability to supply. This leads us to notice an extremely significant discontinuity in the spectrum of channel choices—the space between the high end of retail, say $10,000, and the low end of direct sales, say $75,000. What goes in between?

VAR-Land or No-Man's Land?

Today, the domain between $10,000 and $75,000 is where the structural problem in high-tech distribution is taking its greatest toll. Products in this range provide all the challenges of high-priced products and all the margins of low-priced ones. This creates a very painful squeeze on the vendor, and this squeeze is currently driving a brutal shakeout in the computer industry.

The most visible product line caught in this squeeze is the departmental system designed for the commercial market. Traditionally Unix-based, this has now been reconfigured around an NT-based server, but that has not alleviated the pricing problem, for the total investment required still falls squarely in the middle of the structural gap. Approaching from the bottom end, there is no way the traditional retail channel can provide the services and support needed to install and maintain such systems. Coming from the high end, there is no way that a traditional direct sale and services channel can pay back its cost of servicing such small deals. This is not to say that there is no channel for products in the $10,000 to $75,000 price point. The channel is there— it is the VAR channel. It has the expertise to solve the whole product problem. And it has the low overhead to live with tight pricing margins. Indeed, it is a perfect fit. So what's the problem?

The first problem is that developing this market requires marketing, and *few VARs have either the resources or the inclination to do any marketing.* That is, the marketing position in a VAR organization is frequently staffed as a part-time task for the administrative assistant. VARs tend to market instead based on the Rolodexes of the president and one or more senior salespeople. And once those Rolodexes have been worked over, these companies often go out of business.

The solution to this problem, shockingly, is the product vendors who are seeking to leverage the VAR channel need to provide the channel with their marketing programs, even though the channel knows the target market far better than the vendor. It is a matter of capital and marketing expertise, however, not customer intimacy. Companies who count on VARs to develop or make a market for them simply lose out. Needless to say, the cost of developing and fielding these programs needs to be factored in to the cost of the VAR channel overall, which begins to lessen its apparent cost-effectiveness.

The second problem is *there are not enough VARs to go around,* and their geographic range tends to be at the city level, so that building a nationwide program is a major undertaking that will offer patchy results for years before it can be brought to order. If the market lasts long enough, this investment can be recouped, sometimes dramatically, as in the case of Novell in the 1980s and 3Com in the 1990s. But if VARs are going to be a transitional channel, the geographic model takes too much work. In this situation, one is far better off with a vertical industry model, where a single VAR typically has regional range, and two or three good VARs can cover most of the country.

A third problem with the VAR channel is that, *because its best margins come from labor, not product, it tends to sell enough to fill its plate and then stops selling until it gets hungry again.* That is, like any labor-intensive business, once backlog gets to a certain level, the management of the firm tends to focus on working off the backlog rather than getting more new business. This is not the way either a direct sales force or a retail operation works. In both of those cases, the more you sell, the more you want to sell. From a product supplier's point of view, in other words, VAR distribution is an inherently inefficient mechanism, one that resists its own momentum.

There is a corollary to this principle. VARs tend to be people who perceive themselves not as salespeople but as problem solvers. Often technical in orientation, they perceive selling as a necessary evil, what you have to do in order to get the "real work." This service-oriented rather than sales-oriented self-perception results in a channel that is not very good at selling, further contributing to its inefficiency.

For all these reasons, *VARs are problematic as mainstream distribution channels.* They are best used to support product lines that are forever dedicated to niche markets, ideally vertical niches, where the VARs lack of marketing programs are balanced, over time, by their word-of-mouth reputation in the niche. Autodesk has been and continues to be successful with VARs in architecture, engineering, and construction. Silicon Graphics has had success in Hollywood, Adobe in publishing and graphics, and ESRI is geographic data systems. They also can be useful during rapid market expansions into small business sectors where the customers simply cannot do even the most basic IT work themselves—the Worldwide Web being the most dramatic current example, beginning with a website and then moving up to email and beyond. But because of their inherent instability as an institution, their lack of strong financial underpinnings, and their lack of marketing, they are not normally appropriate as a mainstream market channel.

Adaptations and Alternatives

In this category go the remaining distribution alternatives, which include systems integrators, super-VARs, affiliates, OEMs, selling partnerships, outbound retail, and VADs. From a chasm perspective, each is either inappropriate or too specialized to warrant a lot of attention.

Systems Integrators

These companies have had a long history in the federal government market, where the customer needed all of the advantages of a direct sales relationship, but could not promise a de facto uncompetitive procurement relationship. This meant there was no one to hold accountable for overall systems success. Into this gap entered companies like Electronic Data Systems and Computer Science Corporation.

As the concept of mission-critical systems crossed over from the world of NASA to the world of Fortune 500 boardrooms, commercial America began to take on projects that posed a similar class of problems. At this point, what used to be called the Big Eight firms began to get involved, led by Arthur Anderson. In general, they focus on servicing early market opportunities sponsored by visionary customers, a venue in which systems integrators shine. That is, they run in advance of the institutionalization of the whole product and promise to confer strategic advantage on those customers hardy enough to brave the new technologies.

Because they do not serve pragmatist customers, on the other hand, they are not suitable as a prime channel for crossing the chasm.

Systems integrators are, however, an important part of a mainstream marketing program. This is because the design decisions made in the superprojects can set the procurement agenda for years to come. If the State of California outsources its Worldwide Web infrastructure to EDS, and EDS designs in Sun Sparcstations as its intranet server infrastructure, you can count on a whole lot of Sparcstations being sold over the next five to ten years. How do you win such design-ins?

Systems integrators divide up their product decisions into three buckets. In the first are the technology-critical components. These can sometimes be early-market offers that are the only ones that can enable the system to achieve its goals. Here the integrator takes great risk, does major due diligence, and seeks a *partner relationship* with the provider. In the second bucket are the system-critical platforms, the elements that must be robust and come with strong back-up and support. Here integrators seek out a major systems supplier to help bear this load, typically a market leader with strong enterprise qualifications, as an HP, an IBM, a Compaq, or a Sun, and they are looking for a strong *vendor relationship* with this provider. Finally, any system drags with it an enormous amount of generic purchasing. Here the integrator is not seeking lowest price so much as lowest hassle factor, and they are looking for a really good *supplier relationship.*

The key to winning business with integrators in general is to appreciate what bucket you have been put in and to play that role to perfection. In the case of chasm-crossing products, the only bucket that makes sense is the first one. Here the integrator will put you through hell because the company is afraid you will default on your commitments. Moreover, the bidding processes they want you to support will exhaust what little bandwidth you have for "big deal support." Nonetheless, *because such design-ins can accelerate mainstream market acceptance dramatically, it is critical for companies crossing the chasm to work in cooperation with systems integrators.*

Unfortunately, most marketing organizations lump this assignment in with VAR and OEM sales, and assign a quota to the whole mix, thereby creating an absolutely indigestible clump of work. As was said earlier, systems integrators are not a channel. They do not sell the same thing twice. They are better viewed as an agent of the customer, and they should be served by a direct sales effort on a project-specific basis by senior executives in the vendor firm. They are not suitable for servicing through normal direct sales, because the length of the sales cycle is typically too long, the probability of winning the deal too low, the likelihood of being kept in the deal after it has been won too uncertain, the ultimate payoff too far out in the future, and the special considerations asked inappropriate for anyone but a senior executive in the firm to grant.

It turns out that the most important marketing contribution to ensuring effective working relationships with systems integrators is a communications task, not a selling one. Commercial systems integrators are typically organized in a partnership structure for selling and doing the business, supported by a centralized advanced technology center. The marketing organization's role should be to keep the centralized organization up to speed on any advanced products it is bringing to market, and to develop partner-level communications access for early warning of emerging customer opportunities.

Super-VARs

Super-VARs are a channel that is proposed from time to time for markets which need value-added services to be consistently provided across a broad geography into a cost-sensitive category. The idea is to "roll up" through a series of acquisitions a VAR network that extends nationwide, with a common marketing front end and a single unified back office.

The target customers for this channel are the pragmatist buyers in medium to large-scale companies. These buyers want the security of working with a well-funded organization. Further, they may well have nationwide service issues, so that the LAN they build for the first installation in Pennsylvania may need to be replicated in Alabama and Wisconsin. Most VARs simply cannot operate on a nationwide service basis. Further, on occasion pragmatist buyers will want access to advanced technological expertise. No single VAR can expect to cover the wide breadth of technologies at stake, but a network of many VARS, each contributing its own distinctive expertise, could. Finally, as we noted, local VARs are not as a rule very good marketing organizations. But a national company could invest in marketing expertise, take the demand creation "selling" off the VAR's plate, and leave that organization with the demand fulfillment and service roles for which it is so well suited.

Overall then, the idea is to address some of the inherent limitations in the VAR channel. *On paper the super-VAR channel looks like it should work. School is still out as to whether it makes out in the marketplace.* If it does, this could become an extremely important new channel, especially for the trying-to-emerge client/server market.

OEMs

The logic of an OEM channel is particularly attractive for a small company seeking to do business with hard-nosed pragmatist customers. Why not leverage the direct sales force of an established player in the market?

The difficulty here is in winning the attention of the OEM with a product that requires some creative selling. Demand creation requires sales force focus. The OEM sales force, however, is likely to be focused on the big-ticket products that come out of the company's own R&D labs, not the add-on product coming in from another vendor. Only when that add-on product is sufficiently in demand that its inclusion becomes a deal winner—or the lack of it a deal breaker—will the channel work on the supplier's behalf. That is never going to be the case for a chasm product. *Because it has no patience for the special demands of a chasm product, therefore, the OEM channel is not suited to solving the chasm distribution problem.*

Selling Partnerships

Selling partnerships is not really an industry term, but they are a key tactic in crossing the chasm. The idea is to take the attractiveness of the OEM channel—the notion of leveraging an established relationship with a pragmatist mainstream customer—while recognizing the limited attention one can command in someone else's sales force.

The basic tactic is to cosell with a whole product partner, fielding a direct sales force yourself, sharing leads with the partner, each bringing the other in to help develop comprehensive whole product proposals. In its most noncommittal form, this is not a particularly powerful relationship, but it can be highly leveraged if the chasm-crossing partner devotes resources to evangelizing and educating the other partner's sales force. The key is to simplify the selling arguments so that the partner's sales force has one or two key points to make, generating little subsequent debate from the customer, enough to create an entry point, but not enough to overburden or risk the sale. The right kind of simplification is not always obvious, and it tends to evolve over the life of the product, so success in this tactic requires an ongoing commitment of marketing resources.

Overall, selling partnerships are a transitional strategy that must ultimately resolve into one or another of the stable mainstream-channel alternatives. The reason for this has to do with price. The established partner in this relationship is not wiling to introduce another player who has a product that will soak up a lot of the dollars in the procurement. Basically, if the other product costs more than 15 to 20 percent of the established product, there is too great a perceived risk that the price of the total solution will get out of control. That puts some kind of relative cap on the price of product to which this tactic can be applied. At the same time, this is a very high-cost method of selling, consisting essentially not only of a direct sales force but also the marketing support needed for an indirect one. This puts more pressure on price margins, given the relative price cap, than a company can sustain over time. *Selling partnerships, in other words, are good for priming the pump, but not for the long term.*

Outbound Retail

How do you provide the benefits of a retail channel to someone who does not want to go to the store? Well, if you are Domino's Pizza, you build a franchise based on home delivery. That, in essence, is what outbound retail is all about.

Pragmatist customers, particularly at a Fortune 500 account, want to buy certain types of high-tech products in volume from direct sales representatives who call on them—at least initially—

and then go on to deal with the purchasing department. For these purchase decisions, they do not need a consultative sales process, however, nor do they want to pay the heavy margins associated with this type of channel. Outbound sales forces from retail outlets meet these criteria.

Outbound retail sales forces, however, do not meet the chasm criteria. Although they are organized and managed like a direct sales force, they are not consultative, and therefore they are not demand creators. They are demand fulfillers. That is the way their compensation works, and that is all that the price margins on their products can sustain. A chasm product is a nuisance to them. It generates a disproportionately large amount of explanation to generate a disproportionately small amount of revenue.

The Internet

As a future channel of distribution, the Internet represents the most significant change in computing to date, and maybe ever. It promises to reengineer all other forms of commerce, not eliminating them, nor even disintermediating them, but simply reconstructing them to incorporate its phenomenal reach and service capabilities. Moreover, for early-market offers targeted at technology enthusiasts, the Internet is a superb channel, for it gives visibility to no-name companies at very low cost. All that being said, what can the Internet do for a fledgling enterprise seeking to crossing the chasm?

In general, the answer is, not much as a sales channel. Crossing the chasm requires face-to-face meetings with the target customer to help diagnose their problem and prescribe a heretofore unavailable solution. There is a lot of *orientation* to get through, and live dialogue is the only medium that can make that work. Moreover, post-sales services are always a significant component of a chasm-crossing whole product, which means the sales channel has to be able to show and supervise the results. This undercuts the whole economic model of the Internet, which is to be "hands free" in its offers.

But while the Net is not the sales channel of choice, it can give a strong assist to coordinating the whole product team and to keeping in touch with the target segment. And if the target segment is itself coming together around Internet sites, in the manner, for example, that VerticalNet is trying to orchestrate, then pre-sales services can also get a big boost from the medium.

In sum, it is hard to imagine going to market in high tech without making the Internet medium part of your marketing mix. *But for direct sales of chasm-crossing offers, you can ignore this channel entirely.*

So What's the Right Choice?

The right choice of distribution channel for crossing the chasm is to

1. Use direct sales and support as a demand-creation channel to penetrate the initial target segment and then,
2. Once the segment has become aware of your presence and leadership, to transition to the most efficient fulfillment channel for your offer.

The reason you should always start with direct sales is that time to establish a sustainable market position, and not cost or breadth of sales, is your critical success factor. You simply cannot afford to lose one day of opportunity, and the only channel that would be ever be that responsive to your needs is your own. Moreover, until you have made a market, and can make it clear to others that you have done so, no one has a strong vested interest in supporting your sales. You start the fire.

Once the fire is lit, however, then your job is to spread it as rapidly as possible. This is a totally different problem, and often the people that are good at the one are not good at, indeed often resist transition to, the other. The key here is channel management, beginning with selecting the appropriate channel, then deploying it broadly enough but not too broadly, making sure that channel partners are getting good business, and growing forward accordingly. To be sure, if the market transitions into a hypergrowth mass market, you will have to go through another set of channel strategy decisions, but for the moment, as long as you need strong cooperation from your channel partners to deliver the whole product, it is better to be a little underdistributed to protect their profit margins, than to get overdistributed and have them either drop out or begin to cut corners in their delivery.

This last concern leads us to the final element in our go-to-market checklist, pricing.

Distribution-Oriented Pricing

Pricing decisions are among the hardest for management groups to reach consensus on. The problem is that there are so many perspectives competing for the controlling influence. In this section we are going to sort out some of those perspectives and set out some rational guidelines for pricing during the chasm period.

Customer-Oriented Pricing

The first perspective to set on pricing is the customers', and, as we noted in the section on discovering the chasm, that varies dramatically with their psychographics. Visionaries—the customers dominating the early market's development—are relatively price-insensitive. Seeking a strategic leap forward, with an order-of-magnitude return on investment, they are convinced that any immediate costs are insignificant when compared with the end result. Indeed, they want to make sure there is, if anything, *extra money* in the price, because they know they are going to need special service, and they want their vendors to have the money to provide it. There is even a kind of prestige in buying the high-priced alternative. All this is pure *value-based pricing.* Because of the high value placed on the end result, the product price has a high umbrella under which it can unfold itself.

At the other end of the market are the conservatives. They want low pricing. They have waited a long time before buying the product—long enough for complete institutionalization of the whole product, and long enough for prices to have dropped to only a small margin above cost. This is their reward for buying late. They don't get competitive advantage, but they do keep their out-of-pocket costs way down. This is *cost-based pricing*, something which will eventually emerge in any mainstream market, once all the other margin-justifying elements have been exhausted.

Between these two types lie the pragmatists—our target customers for the chasm-crossing effort. Pragmatists, as we have said repeatedly, want to back the market leader. They have learned that by so doing they can keep their whole product costs—the costs not only of purchase but of ownership as well—to their lowest, and still get some competitive leverage from the investment. They expect to pay a premium price for the market leader relative to the competition, perhaps as high as 30 percent. This is *competition-based pricing*. Even though the market leaders are getting a premium, their allowed price is still a function of comparison with the other players in the market. And if they are not the market leader, they will have to apply the reverse of this rule and discount accordingly.

From the customer perspective, then, as we argued in the previous chapter, the key issue is market leadership versus a viable competitive set, and the key pricing strategy is premium margin above a norm set by comparison.

Vendor-Oriented Pricing

Vendor-oriented pricing is a function of internal issues, beginning with cost of goods, and extending to cost of sales, cost of overhead, cost of capital, promised rate of return, and any number of other factors. These factors are critical to being able to manage an enterprise profitably on an ongoing basis. None of these, however, has any immediate meaning in the marketplace. They take on meaning only as they impact other market-visible issues.

For example, vendor-oriented pricing typically sets the distribution channel decision by establishing a price-point ballpark that puts the product in the direct sales, retail, or VAR camp. Moreover, once the product is in the market, vendor-oriented factors can make a big impact if, for example, they allow us a low-cost pricing advantage in a late mainstream market, or if they allow us to use operating margins to fund new R&D for the next early market.

Vendor-oriented pricing, however, represents the worst basis for pricing decisions during the chasm period. This is a time when we must be almost entirely external focused—both on the new demands of the mainstream customer and the new relationship we are trying to build with a mainstream channel. Indeed, because of the primary importance of securing ongoing means of access to the mainstream, this latter issue should be the number-one factor for pricing decisions during this period.

Distribution-Oriented Pricing

From a distribution perspective, there are two pricing issues that have significant impact on channel motivation:

- Is it priced to sell?
- Is it worthwhile to sell?

Being priced to sell means that price does not become a major issue during the sales cycle. Companies crossing the chasm, coming from success in the early market with visionary customers, typically have their products priced too high. Price does become an issue with the pragmatist customer, but when the channel feeds back prospect resistance and uses comparable products as evidence of the expected pricing, companies too often argue that they have no such competition, and that the channel does not know how to sell the product properly.

However, products can also be priced too low to cross the chasm. The problem here is that the price does not incorporate a sufficient margin to reward the channel for its extra effort in introducing this novelty into their already established relationship with the mainstream customer. If the channel is going to go out of its way to take on something new, the reward has to be significantly more attractive than whatever is available from business as usual.

If we put all these perspectives together and look at them in a crossing-the-chasm context, the fundamental pricing goal should be as follows: *Set pricing at the market leader price point, thereby reinforcing your claims to market leadership (or at least not undercutting them), and build a disproportionately high reward for the channel into the price margin, a reward that will be phased out as the product becomes truly established in the mainstream, and competition for the right to distribute it increases.*

Recap: Invasion Launching

To sum up, the last step in the D-Day strategy for crossing the chasm is launching the invasion—that is, putting a price on your product and putting it into a sales channel. Neither of these actions resolves itself readily into a checklist of activities, but there are four key principles to guide us:

1. The prime goal is to secure access to a customer-oriented distribution channel. This is the channel you predict that mainstream pragmatist customers would want and expect to buy your product from.
2. The type of channel you select for long-term servicing of the market is a function of the price point of the product. If this is not direct sales, however, then during the transition period of crossing the chasm, you may need to adopt a supplementary or even an alternative channel—one oriented toward demand creation—to stimulate early acceptance in the mainstream.
3. Price in the mainstream market carries a message, one that can make your product easier—or harder—to sell. Since the only acceptable message is one of market leadership, your price needs to convey that, which makes it a function of the pricing of comparable products in your identified competitive set.
4. Finally, you must remember that margins are the channel's reward. Since crossing the chasm puts extra pressure on the channel, and since you are often trying to leverage the equity the channel has in its existing relationships with pragmatist customers, you should pay a premium margin to the channel during the chasm period.

This list of principles not only concludes this chapter but ties together chapters 3 through 7 on marketing strategy for crossing the chasm. The goal of these chapters has been to lay out a framework of marketing ideas to assist companies in meeting the challenges of the chasm period. The D-Day strategy, as a whole, seeks to emphasize both the great peril and the great opportunity that lie before a company in this situation. The greatest impediment to action in such situations is often a lack of understanding of the appropriate alternatives. Hopefully, these chapters have gone some distance toward removing that impediment.

Having said all that, there is, finally, a larger set of issues that come into play. For if the chasm is a great challenge—and it is—it is one that is in large part self-imposed. To put it simply, our industry makes the chasm worse than it has to be. Until we understand how we do so, and stop doing so, we will never really master the chasm.

With this thought in mind, let us turn to our conclusion, "Leaving the Chasm Behind."

Conclusion

Getting Beyond the Chasm

It has become very fashionable of late to talk about how high-tech companies can and should become market-driven organizations. My own view, however, is that there is not any *becoming* involved. All organizations *are* market-driven, whether they acknowledge it or not. The chasm phenomenon—the rapid acceleration in market development followed by a dramatic lull, occurring whenever a discontinuous innovation is introduced—drives all emerging high-tech enterprises to a point of crisis where they must leave the relative safety of their established early market and go out in search of a new home in the mainstream. These forces are inexorable—they *will* drive the company. The key question is whether the management can become aware of the changes in time to leverage the opportunities such awareness confers.

Thus far we have been treating the chasm as a market development problem and have focused exclusively on marketing strategies and tactics for crossing it. But the impact of the chasm extends beyond the marketing organization to every other aspect of the high-tech enterprise. In this final chapter, therefore, we are going to step back from the marketing view and look at three

other critical arenas of change: finance, organizational development, and R&D. The goal of the discussion in every case is the
same—to keep the enterprise moving forward into the mainstream marketplace and not, as so often happens, to allow it to
fall back into the chasm.

The fundamental lesson of this chapter is a simple one: *The
postchasm enterprise is bound by the commitments made by the prechasm enterprise.* These prechasm commitments, made in haste
during the flurry of just trying to get a foothold in an early market, are all too frequently simply unmaintainable in the new situation. That is, they promise a level of performance or reward that,
if delivered, would simply destroy the enterprise. This means
that all too often one of the first tasks of the postchasm era is to
manage our way out of the contradictions imposed by prechasm
agreements. This, in turn, can involve a major devaluation of the
assets of the enterprise, significant demotions for people who are
unsuited to the responsibilities implied by their titles, and
marked changes in authority over the future of the product and
technology—all of which is likely to end in bitter disappointments and deep-seated resentment. In short, it can be a very nasty
period indeed.

The first and best solution to this class of problems is to avoid
them altogether—that is, *to avoid making the wrong kind of commitments during the prechasm period.* By looking ahead at the outset,
while we are still in the early market phase, to where we must go
in order to survive the chasm crisis, we can vaccinate ourselves
against making the kind of crippling decisions that doom so
many otherwise promising high-tech enterprises.

Let me acknowledge that this is much harder to achieve than
it looks. I am reminded of the many times as an adolescent when
I was sagely advised that I was in the process of making some
very bad decisions because I was "going through a phase." I
loathed that advice. First, it made me feel vaguely inadequate
and rather inferior to the person giving it. And second, even
though I suspected it to be true, it was totally useless information.
I might be going through a phase, but since I was in the phase,
and was therefore doomed to perform in some incompetent way,
what good was this knowledge? How could I stop being myself?

That, however, is exactly what the high-tech enterprise must
accomplish to leave the chasm behind. The enterprise must stop

"being itself"—in the sense that it must accept that it is going through a phase and act competently with that knowledge.

To leave the chasm behind, there is a molting process that must occur, a change of company self, wherein we grow away from celebrating familial feelings and dashing individual performances and step toward rewarding predictable, orchestrated group dynamics. It is not a time to cease innovation or to sacrifice creativity. But there is a call to redirect that energy toward the concerns of a pragmatist's value system instead of a visionary's. It is not a time to forgo friendships and implement an authoritarian management regime. Indeed, management style is one of the few things that can remain constant during this period of transition. But there is a call to review and revalue the skills and instincts and talents that helped to build up a leadership in the early market in light of the new challenge of building leadership in the mainstream. And that call can and will test friendships and egos throughout the firm.

The principles and practices for successful postchasm management of financial, organizational, and product development issues are all significantly different from their prechasm counterparts, and not everyone is adaptable or amenable to the changes required to operate in the new order. The good news is, in either case, there will always be plenty of jobs. That is, while individual high-tech enterprises have shown a very erratic track record over the past 10 years, the sum total of revenue and employment of the industry as a whole has grown dramatically. We all need to remember this during the chasm reshuffling. It should not be our goal, that is, to try to evangelize a new style of behavior but rather to create a framework for helping individuals understand for themselves where they best fit in, and then take appropriate action.

With that thought in mind, let us turn to the first and most influential set of decisions that postchasm enterprises inherit from their prechasm selves—the financial ones.

Financial Decisions: Breaking the Hockey Stick

The purpose of the postchasm enterprise is *to make money*. This is a much more radical statement than it appears. To begin with, we need to recognize that this is not the purpose of the prechasm organization. In the case of building an early market, the fundamental return on investment is the conversion of an amalgam of technology, services, and ideas into a replicable, manufacturable product and the proving out that there is some customer demand for this product. Early market revenues are the first measure of this demand, but they are typically not—nor are they expected to be—a source of profit. As a result, the early market organization is not required to adopt the discipline of profitability.

Nor does the prechasm organization motivate itself by profitability, or typically any other financial goal. Oh, to be sure, there are the get-rich dreams that float in and out of idle conversation. But there are much headier rewards closer at hand—the freedom to be your own boss and chart your own course—the chance to explore the leading edge of some new technology, the career-opening opportunity to take on far more responsibility than any established organization would ever grant. These are what really drive early market organizations to work such long hours for such modest rewards—the dream of getting rich on equity is only an excuse, something to hold out to your family and friends as a rationale for all this otherwise crazy behavior.

So early market entrepreneurs are not called to focus on, nor are they oriented toward, making money. This has enormous significance, as most management theory assumes a profit motive present, serving as a corrective check against otherwise alluring tactics. When that motive is not present, people make financial commitments that have consequences they either do not, or do not care to, foresee. Although this comes in many and varied forms, perhaps its most prevalent one is the *hockey stick forecast of revenue growth.*

In the current, flawed model of high-tech market development—the two-stage one without the chasm—the entrepreneur is asked to drive the enterprise to an early market success and then to hand over the reins to professional managers who will guide the company as its revenues and profits skyrocket toward market leadership. This is the model traditionally endorsed by the venture capital community, the one it uses to attract its capital funds, and the one it applies to its investment opportunities. If you do not show this kind of meteoric rate of return sooner or later, you are not qualified to participate in their portfolio.

Entrepreneurs may be many things when it comes to financial issues, but they are typically not slow on the uptake. If venture capitalists are the ones with the money, and these are the rules you follow to get that money, then they will be sure to follow the rules. And so entrepreneurs raise capital using "hockey stick" graphs of revenue attainment. That is, they bring forward a business plan that shows no revenue development for some period of time—as long as they possibly can defer—after which there is a sharp inflection in the curve, and rapid, continuous, and what any sane person would call miraculous, revenue growth from there on. As a form, it is as precise and conventional as a love sonnet—and just as likely to get one into trouble.

Hockey stick curves are created by spreadsheets, a software tool that many have argued has driven some of the worst of the investment decisions of the past two decades. It is so easy to increment a revenue number by a percentage and just let the software take it from there. Now in theory, this revenue line approximates a real profile of how the company could capitalize on a developing market opportunity. As such, it would serve as the "master line" in the spreadsheet, the one to which all others must account. That is how profitable operations work.

In fact, however, the revenue line is a slave—and to not just one but two masters. At the front end, it is slave to the entrepreneur's cost curve, and at the back, to the venture capitalist's hockey stick expectations. Revenue numbers, under this methodology, are . . . well, whatever they have to be. Once that sum is identified, then market analyst reports are scoured for some appropriate citations, and any other source of evidence or credibility is enlisted, to justify what is a fundamentally arbitrary and unjustifiable projection of revenue growth.

Now, if the current model of high-tech market development were not flawed, this might work, or at least work better or more often. But in fact, the revenue development that actually occurs looks more like a *staircase* than a hockey stick. That is, there is an initial period of rapid revenue growth, representing the development of the early market, followed by a period of slow to no growth (the chasm period), followed by a second phase of rapid growth, representing return on one's initial mainstream market development. This staircase can continue indefinitely, with the flat periods representing slower growth due to transitioning into broader and broader mainstream segments, and the rapid rises representing the ability to capitalize on those efforts. As more and more segments are served, sooner or later the ups and downs begin to cancel each other out, and one can achieve the less bumpy results that Wall Street greatly prefers. (In fact, only the most successful high-tech companies have achieved such a state; most continue to fluctuate more dramatically than the financial community can understand, with the result that their stocks routinely take a vicious beating at the slightest indication of bad news.)

All this is well and good. The staircase model is perfectly viable—unless you have mortgaged your stake in the company on making the hockey stick scenario come true. That, unfortunately, is precisely what most high-tech funding plans commit to. And when the hockey stick scenario does not come true, and the mortgage comes due, the founder's equity gets radically diluted, things fall apart, and the company dies in the chasm. That is the course sketched out in the high-tech parable in Chapter 1 of this book.

Now, the venture community has long been aware of this problem. Cynics in high tech believe they count on it—that's how the "vulture capitalists" take over the company from the unwitting entrepreneur. But the truth is, such a strategy is a lose/lose proposition, and most investors know it. They may call it "the valley of death" instead of the chasm, but they know it is there. All they have to do is look at their own portfolios.

The question now becomes, if we have the chasm model to work with, what can we do differently? This question really breaks into two parts—one directed to the financial communities that provide the sources of capital, and the other to the high-tech executives who provide the sources of management. For the former, the key issue is how to reformulate its concepts of valuation and expected rate of return, and for the latter, it is when to spend capital and when to adopt the discipline of profitability. Let's look at both of these more closely.

The Role of the Venture-Financing Community

All investment is a bet on performance against competition within time. What the chasm model surfaces is a need to rethink these variables. From the investment point of view, the most pressing question initially is, How wide is the chasm? Or, to put this in investment terms, How long will it take before I can achieve a reasonably predictable ROI from an acceptably large mainstream market?

The simple answer to this question is, as long as it takes to create and install a sustainable whole product. The chasm model asserts that no mainstream market can occur until the whole product is in place. A reasonable corollary, I believe, is that once the whole product is in place—in other words, has become institutionalized—the market will develop quickly—normally, although not necessarily, around the company that drove and led the whole product effort.

Can we predict how long this will take? I think so. By analyzing the target customer and the compelling reason to buy, and then dissecting all the components of the whole product, we can reduce this process to a manageable set of performance factors, each of which can be projected ahead in time, with an estimated point of convergence. It's not a science, but it's not a black art either: It is, in essence, just another kind of business plan.

Supposing this plan has some credibility, a raft of other questions immediately follow. How big will this market be? Again, the simple answer is, As big as can be motivated by the value proposition—the compelling reason to buy—and served by the whole product. Market boundaries occur, in other words, at the point of failure of either the value proposition or the whole product. The other market-making factors—alliances, competition, positioning, distribution, and pricing—do not impact the size of market but rather the rate of market penetration. Given free market economy incentives, efficient solutions in these areas will fall into place sooner or later if the market is truly there.

If all of the preceding assertions are true—and that is certainly something that warrants further investigation—then all the key factors of the investment decision are reasonably out in the open, and the decision itself can be made without having to consult the entrails of a sacrificial animal. Estimates of market size, rate of penetration, cost to achieve market leadership, and anticipated market share can all be made in the light of day, without smoke and without mirrors. There will still be plenty of room for disagreement about probability of success and degree of risk, but there should not be any fundamental leap of faith demanded, no "drinking of the Kool-Aid" as one of my more macabre colleagues has put it.

So the call to action to the investment community is, Make your client companies incorporate crossing the chasm into their business planning. Demand to see not only broad, long-term market characterizations but also specific target customers for the D-Day attack. Drive them to refine their value propositions until they are truly compelling, and then use these to test how many target customers there truly are. Force them to define the whole product, and then help them to build relationships with the right partners and allies. Again, use the results to test hypotheses about market size. As for competitive set and positioning, beware of pushing your small fishes too soon into big ponds. And as for distribution and pricing, don't look for "standard margins" until the chasm has truly been crossed. To sum up, use the crossing-the-chasm matrix of ideas to ensure proper management of financial assets.

The Role of the Venture-Managing Community

Now let's turn to the entrepreneur's key concern: How long should I live off of capital, and when should I adopt the discipline of profitability? The bounds of this decision work as follows. Until profitability is achieved, nothing is secure, and your destiny is not under your own control. This argues for early adoption. In fact, in slow-developing markets, particularly in the software industry, which has low capitalization requirements, there is a very strong case for adopting profitability from day one. Early visionary customers will pay consulting fees and prepay royalties to help fund low capitalization start-ups. From an accounting view, these prepaid royalties cannot be booked immediately as revenue, but they can make you cash-flow positive from day one, and thus keep 100 percent of the equity reserved for a later date.

The great benefit of adopting the discipline of profitability at the outset is that you do not have to learn it later on. All too frequently, even when they are led by experienced managers, enterprises that are funded for long periods of time fall into a "welfare state mentality," losing their sense of urgency, and looking for their next paycheck to come from yet another round of financing instead of from the marketplace. Moreover, the discipline of profitability teaches you to "just say no" early and often. For most ideas there simply isn't any money to fund them. The enterprise is forced to focus drastically just because of resource constraints. This radically reduces time to market because people are not focused on doing something else and because they understand it is the market that is paying their paychecks. And finally, when one does go seeking external capital, there is no stronger evidence for a high company valuation than it having already demonstrated not only real market demand but its own ability to process that demand profitably.

Indeed, the case for seeking profitability from the beginning is so strong, you begin to wonder why you would ever not choose this route. Essentially, there are two reasons. First, the price of entry is too great to fund with sweat equity or consulting contracts. This is clearly the case in any manufacturing-intensive operation. Today, however, with the move to outsourced manufacturing, when companies like Cisco ship as much as 45% of their products *without ever touching them,* when fabless semiconductor companies use foundries for all their goods, and when there is even such a thing as a chipless semiconductor company, Rambus, which simply licenses a patented memory interface architecture, it is more a matter of getting the team on board and the engineering in place than it is putting in place a line or ramping up inventory. Still, there are real costs here that typically well exceed a pay-as-you-go budget, and a lot of venture funding goes to supporting just this sort of enterprise.

The other reason to forego initial profitability is when the market is expected to develop so rapidly that you cannot afford to mark time as a bit player. The explosion of the Internet has created a land-grab mentality heretofore unknown, and everyone is racing to beat out competitors in capturing market share. Yahoo!'s capturing the number one position in search sites, Amazon.com's achievement in book reselling, and America Online's in-home communications, all have translated into dramatic surges in market capitalization that have left their competitors seemingly permanently behind. In that kind of game, the race really is to the swiftest, and second prize is a long way back from first, so spending early and big is seen as the key to success. (I personally am extremely nervous about such blind-leading-the-blind markets, but then I am a late adopter by nature.)

Beyond this there is a third, more general principle that can help entrepreneurs think through their management of capital. It is typically more capital intensive to cross the chasm than it is to build the early market. Early market development efforts typically do not respond well to massive infusions of capital—in the 1980s we saw this with the IBM PC Jr. and Prodigy; in the 1990s with pen-based computers and video-to-the-home. You simply cannot spend your way into the hearts and minds of technology enthusiasts and visionaries. To be sure, there is a minimum level of capitalization required. You have to be able to travel to make direct sales calls, and show up looking presentable, and you probably should have an office and a phone that is answered in a professional way. You do need to invest in early market public relations—the product launch is crucial to building early market success—but you do not need to advertise, nor do you need to invest in developing partnerships or building channel relationships. All this is premature until you have established some early market credibility on your own.

Once early market leadership has been established, however, the entire equation changes. The whole product investment—securing the partnerships and alliances and then making them work to deliver the final goods—takes a significant number of funded initiatives. So does the channel development process, both on the pull and on the push sides, creating demand and providing incentives for sales. And it is critical during this period to have an effective communications program, including press relations, market relations, and advertising.

In sum, this is when you want to spend your money—not before. It is important, therefore, that you not start this process until after you have established early market leadership, and that you not commit to throwing off all kinds of cash during the chasm period. Simply applying these two concepts to the business plan can keep you out of a lot of trouble.

Organizational Decisions: From Pioneers to Settlers

Turning from issues of finance to issues of people, we must recognize that the chasm separates not only visionaries from pragmatists—it also separates the companies that serve them. To leave the chasm behind, to cross it and not fall back into it, involves a transformation in the enterprise that few individuals can span. *It is the move from being pioneers to becoming settlers.*

In the development organization, pioneers are the ones who push the edge of the technology application envelope. They do not institutionalize. They do not like to create infrastructure. They don't even like to document. They want to do great deeds, and when there are no more great deeds to be done, they want to move on. Their brilliance fuels the early market, and without them, there would be no such thing as high tech.

Nonetheless, once you have crossed the chasm, these people can become a potential liability. Their fundamental interest is to innovate, not administrate. Things like industry standards and common interfaces and adaptations to installed solutions, even when these solutions are clearly technically inferior, are all foreign and repugnant to the high-tech pioneers. So as the market infrastructure begins to close in around them, they are already looking for less crowded country. In the meantime, they are not likely to cooperate in the compromises needed, and can be highly disruptive to groups that are seeking to carry this agenda out. It is critical, therefore, that as the enterprise shifts from the product-centric world of the early market to the market-centric world of the mainstream, that pioneer technologists be transferred else-where—ideally, into another project within the enterprise, but if necessary, to another company.

There is a comparable process going on in the sales force at the same time. Here the group at the forefront is the high-tech sales pioneers. These are people who have the gift of selling to visionaries. They are able to understand the technology and product at a level where they can readily manipulate it and adapt it to the dreams of the visionaries. They can talk the visionaries' language, understand the quantum leap forward visionaries seek to achieve, and wrap their products in that cloak. They can translate that language back into concrete manifestations of the product, to be illustrated through custom demos, for which they make insatiable demands. They can think big, and they can get big orders. They are the darlings of the early market. Without them, achieving early market leadership is all but impossible.

These same people, however, also become a liability once you have crossed the chasm. Indeed, they are the ones primarily responsible for dragging companies back into the chasm. The problem is, they cannot stop making the visionary sale, a sale predicated on delivering custom implementations of the whole product. Such contracts are fulfilled by robbing from Peter—the mainstream R&D effort—to pay Paul—the custom R&D effort necessary to achieve the visionaries' buying objective. The key to leaving the chasm behind, however, is to stop custom developments and institutionalize the whole product, to build to a set of standards that the marketplace as a whole can support. This mainstream effort necessarily puts enormous strain on the R&D department, who must not, therefore, be distracted by yet another wild and crazy venture. And so it is that a pioneer salesperson left unchecked can be highly disruptive and demoralizing to a sales organization looking to leave the chasm behind.

So now we have two sets of people—high-tech pioneers and pioneer salespeople—who are fundamental to success in the early market and potentially a liability after the company has crossed the chasm. They must be outplaced, but who is competent to do so? And how in the world will their knowledge ever be replaced? And who is going to take over what they leave behind? And is any of this moral or fair, given their contributions to date?

I know of no high-tech firm that has not struggled with these issues sooner or later. And how you respond affects not only those who leave but those who stay. This is a time when you must perform impeccably.

Let's deal with the moral issue first. And let us take as our starting point that casting aside people, dislocating their lives and threatening their livelihood, is immoral—even if businesses and governments routinely do so with abandon. The issues then become ones of foresight, agreement, planning, and preparation. Pioneers do not want to settle down. That is not in their best interest nor in the interest of the companies that employ them. If, at the beginning of the process, everyone can acknowledge this fact, and acknowledge that the very goal of pioneers, the final manifestation of their success, is to create a mainstream market and thereby put themselves out of a job, then we can have a reasonable basis for going forward. How we would go forward and under what kind of compensation program is a discussion we need to postpone until we look at how to make the transition to the other side of the equation, to the settlers who are expected to come in and take their place.

The truth is, of course, that settlers do not take pioneers' places. They take other places, ones that pioneers never have occupied nor would ever choose to. Nonetheless, settlers do take over the employment roster, and the management positions and the authority and, ultimately, the budget. And they build fences and create laws (called procedures) and do all the things that created range wars between pioneers and settlers back in the Old West. All this bodes well for the postchasm marketplace, populated with pragmatists, who like reliable, predictable people and abhor surprises. But it hardly sits well with the pioneers. How in the world, then, can you make the transition between these two groups in an orderly way?

Two New Job Descriptions

The key is to initiate the transition by introducing two new roles during the crossing-the-chasm effort. The first of these might be called the *target market segment manager,* and the second, the *whole product manager.* Both are temporary, transitional positions, with each being a stepping stone to a more traditional role. Specifically, the former leads to being an industry marketing manager, and the latter to a product marketing manager. These are their "real titles," the ones under which they are hired, the ones that are most appropriate for their business cards. But during the chasm transition they should be assigned unique, one-time-only responsibilities, and while they are in that mode, we will use their "interim" titles.

The target market segment manager has one goal in his or her short job life—to transform a visionary customer relationship into a potential beachhead for entry into the mainstream vertical market that particular customer participates in. If Citicorp is the client, then it is banking; if Aetna, insurance; if Dupont, chemicals; if Intel, semiconductors. The process works like this.

Once you have closed such an account as part of an early market sales program, assign the target market segment manager as its account manager with a charter that allows him the kind of extensive customer contact that will let him really learn how their business works. He must attend the trade shows, read the literature, study the systems, and meet the people—first, just within the one account, and subsequently, in related companies. At the same time, he must take over the supervision of the visionary's project, make sure it gets broken up into achievable phases, supervise the introduction and rollout of the early phases, get feedback and buy-in from the end users of the system, and work with the in-house staff to spin off the kind of localized implementations that give these initial deliverables immediate value and impact. At the same time, he will be working with the whole product manager to identify which parts of the visionary project are suitable for an ongoing role in the whole product and which are not. The goal is to isolate the idiosyncratic elements as account-specific modifications, making sure thereby not to saddle the ongoing product development team with the burden of maintaining them.

The market segment manager should not be expected to generate additional revenue from the account in the short term, because the visionaries believe they have already paid for every possible modification they might need. What he can be expected to do, however, is the following:

- *Expedite the implementation of the first installation of the system.* This not only contributes to the bottom line, as it will expedite the purchase of additional systems, but it also secures the beginning of a reference base in the target market segment. Most companies fail miserably in this regard, so much so that even several years later their initial "big name" accounts cannot be referenced. The key here is to remember that pragmatists are not interested in hearing about who you have sold to but rather who has a fully implemented system.

- *During the implementation of the first installation, introduce into the account his own replacement, a true account manager, a "setter," who will serve this client, hopefully, for many years to come.* Note that at this point the pioneer salesperson is still in the picture, still has the relationship with the visionary, but that the day-to-day operation of the account is entirely in others' hands. This is typically just fine with the pioneer, for he recognizes this to be the kind of detail-oriented settler work for which he has no liking.

- *Leverage the ongoing project to create one or more whole product extensions that solve some industrywide problem in an elegant way.* The intent is either to absorb these elements into the product line or to distribute them informally as an unsupported product extension through a users' group. Either way, such add-ons increase the value of the product within the target market segment and create a barrier to entry for any other vendor.

The Whole Product Manager

While the target market segment manager is pursuing these tasks in the customer's environment, there is a corresponding internal role to be filled. Here the transition is from product manager to product marketing manager via the short-lived role of whole product manager. These titles are all sufficiently alike as to be confusing, so let's take a minute to sort out these three very different jobs.

A *product manager* is a member of either the marketing organization or the development organization who is responsible for ensuring that a product gets created, tested, and shipped on schedule and meeting specification. It is a highly internally focused job, bridging the marketing and development organizations, and requiring a high degree of technical competence and project management experience.

A *product marketing manager* is always a member of the marketing organization, never of the development group, and is responsible for bringing the product to the marketplace and to the distribution organization. This includes all of the elements on the crossing-the-chasm agenda, from target-customer identification through to pricing. It is a highly externally focused job.

Not all organizations separate product managers from product marketing managers, but they should. Combining the jobs almost always results in one or the other simply not getting done. And the type of people who are good at one are rarely good at the other.

Now, the *whole product manager* is a product-marketing-manager-to-be. The reason she is not one today is that the job itself is premature. Until there is a successful crossing of the chasm, there are no meaningful market relationships or understandings to drive the future of product development. The target market segment manager is off getting these under way, but they are not there today. What is there today, on the other hand, is a list of bug reports and product-enhancement requests that is growing with disconcerting speed. *If this list is not managed properly, it will bring the entire development organization to its knees.*

The tactic, which at once secures proper management of the list and initiates a transition process from pioneer to settler culture in the development side of the house, is to take this list away from the product manager and give it to the whole product manager. For whoever is serving as the product manager at this point almost certainly is a pioneer—otherwise, the organization could not have got to where it is today. The problem with this person continuing to direct the future of the product is that she will be driven first and foremost by her own personal commitments made to early customers. Unfortunately, these commitments are often not in the best interest of the mainstream market customer. To be sure, they must eventually be fulfilled—unless they are to be negotiated away—but in either case, they should not be given automatic priority over other issues. What should increasingly become the prioritizing factor for ongoing product development work is contribution to mainstream, pragmatist customer satisfaction—in other words, contribution to the whole product—hence, the need to transfer authority.

Once this authority is transferred, the enterprise has taken a key step in moving from a product-driven to a market-driven organization. As the shape of the mainstream market emerges, as the needs of this market can be increasingly identified through market research and customer interviews, then the whole product manager steps into the title that she has had all along on her business card, product marketing manager. To try to take this step earlier in the market development cycle is foolish. During the early market it is important to be product-driven and to give strong powers to the product manager. But to fail to take it now is equally foolish, for every day that the enhancement list is in the hands of the original pioneers, the company risks making additional development commitments to unstrategic ends.

To sum up, at the beginning of the chasm period, the organization is dominated by pioneers, with strong powers invested in a few top-gun salespeople and product managers. By the time we are into the mainstream market, that power should be distributed far more broadly among major account managers, industry marketing managers, and product marketing managers. This gradual dissemination of authority will ultimately frustrate the pioneer contributors, hampering their ability to make quick decisions and rapid responses. Ultimately, it will make them want to leave.

Coping with Compensation

This brings us back, full circle, to the fundamental issue that underlies so much of the frustration and disappointment that builds up within high-tech organizations—compensation. Few compensation programs recognize either the fundamentally different contributions of pioneers and settlers or their fundamentally different tenures with the enterprise, and thus these programs end up discriminating against one or the other. And when compensation programs do discriminate—when they discourage the very behaviors that ought to be rewarded, or vice versa—then organizations fail.

To work through all the complexities of designing appropriate compensation schemes is beyond both the scope of this book and the capabilities of its author. I can only sketch out a few general principles that seem important to follow.

First, let's start on the sales side. A typical pioneer sale involves a broad purchase agreement, predicated on successful implementation of a pilot project. Even when there has been a major up-front payment, the rational way to book this business is to defer recognizing the larger order until it has been confirmed. That could be at least a year away, and during that period, we will have introduced a number of new players into the account, including the target market segment manager. The pioneer salesperson might even be gone by then. Say, some account manager just joins the firm, inherits the account, and all of a sudden the flood of orders come in. What is the appropriate way to compensate?

The key is to discriminate between account penetration and account development. The latter is a more predictable, less remarkable achieve-ment. It is also the more lucrative. Compensation here should reward such things as longevity of the relationship, customer satisfaction, and predictability of revenue stream. It should be spread out over time and not clumped into dramatic payments. Because there is high value associated with the intangibles of the ongoing customer relationship, much of it can be based on an MBO formula rather than pure revenue attainment. If equity is part of the compensation strategy for the firm as a whole, it is a reasonable component here as well, provided it is doled out slowly, with the larger portions coming at the end of the program, to reward stability of service. Overall, however, since this is not a high-risk role, it should not be a high-reward one either.

Compensation for the pioneer salesperson should have the opposite characteristics. It should provide the bulk of its rewards immediately, in recognition of a single key achievement—winning the account. This is an extraordinary event, one that few can accomplish, and it is critical to determining the firm's long-term future. It is an extraordinarily high risk endeavor, with the odds stacked heavily against the salesperson. It therefore deserves extraordinary compensation. On the other hand, if it was achieved by promising more than anyone can deliver, perhaps even more than anyone really knew, then that is not behavior we want to reward. So, although we would like the compensation to be front-loaded, there must also be a reality check built into the process. Because the pioneer salesperson will be moving on, we do not want an extended compensation program, and thus equity, for example, is an inappropriate vehicle. Taking all this together, the situation argues for a bonus-based program more than a straight commission approach—something lucrative for the salesperson, event-driven and over and done with relatively quickly, and not so closely tied to revenue recognition that either the pioneer has to overstay his or her welcome in order to reap the rewards or earns an extraordinary cash reward at a time when the company simply cannot afford that sort of outlay.

Compensating Developers

Moving over to the development side, there is one remaining compensation challenge—the pioneer technologist. These divide into two camps—true company founders and very early employees. The former have bet their lives on the equity gamble, and there is nothing further to discuss, except to hope that in reading this book they learn to conserve a large portion of that equity to fund crossing the chasm. The latter pose a real problem. They can point with accuracy to the notion that they created a large part of the core product. Thus, should that product become a mainstream market hit, they feel they should get a major share of the gains. The fact is, they don't, and the truth is, bluntly, they don't deserve it either. Mainstream success, as we have argued at length, is a function of the whole product, not the core product, and that is a very large team effort indeed.

What the pioneer technologist does have a right to is a large share of the early market returns, because here it truly is the core product that drives success. The problem is that cash is typically so tight during this period that there is none to throw off in the form of a reward. So equity is the usual fallback. This is a compromise, to say the least, as equity should be reserved for people who cross the chasm and stay—not the pioneer's ideal role.

The final word on pioneer technologists, I suppose, is that they are in the same bind as authors—a fate I can identify with. Like authors, they are compelled to conduct their craft regardless of whether anyone will pay for it. As such, their negotiating position is fundamentally weak, and their normal compensation reflects it.

To sum up, improper compensation wastes dollars and demotivates people. To be appropriate to high tech, compensation programs must take into account the differences between desired performance in the early market and mainstream market, as well as the types of people that can be called on to achieve these performances, and the likelihood that some of these people will need to leave the company long before it achieves significant profitability. If we can sort through these issues, and come up with an appropriate distribution of rewards, we can forgo much of the agony and loss of momentum that accompany most crossings of the chasm. If we continue to operate the way we do today, we will persist in constructing self-conflicting organizations and wonder why they are not more productive.

R&D Decisions: From Products to Whole Products

At the outset of this book, we set crossing the chasm as the fundamental marketing priority in high tech. In the middle we established that institutionalizing the whole product was the fundamental strategy for succeeding in this endeavor. It is fitting, therefore, to finish up with a look at the impact of whole product marketing on long-term R&D.

R&D is high tech. Everything else is secondary. As an industrial sector, before anything else, we are technology-driven. Eventually we learn to create products, and then markets, and then enterprises to dominate those markets. But it starts with technology. "Build the product and they will come," to paraphrase the theme of the movie *Field of Dreams*. That is our fundamental dream, the dynamic that drives all else.

The problem is, we grow past the dream. The products and markets and companies we create all grow up to make persistent and legitimate demands on us, and we have no choice but to serve them. *And once this scenario begins, R&D doesn't get to focus on the generic product anymore. It must become whole product R&D.*

Whole product R&D is driven not by the laboratory but by the marketplace. It begins not with creative technology but with creative market segmentation. It penetrates not into protons and processes but rather into habits and behaviors. It does not, like the captain of the starship *Enterprise*, "go where no man has gone before," but rather, like T. S. Eliot, finds the end of all its exploring is "to arrive where we started and know the place for the first time." It prefers to assemble its creations from existing technologies and products rather than to invent new ones from scratch. Its heroes are less like Einstein, who developed a whole universe out of his own head, and more like George Washington Carver, who discovered over three hundred different uses for the peanut.

Not very heady stuff. No wonder it is so often ignored. Indeed, the word that high tech uses for whole product R&D is *maintenance*. And the people they assign to it are . . . well, the janitorial types. No top guns want to go near this stuff.

Instead, the top guns rush out to create more discontinuous innovations, flooding the market with far more technology than it can possibly absorb, and complaining all the while about how product life cycles are becoming shorter and shorter. They play the game, in other words, almost entirely to the left of the chasm, cycling though endless repetitions of early markets that never cross over to the mainstream. *Product* life cycles truly are getting shorter—but *whole* product life cycles are as long as they ever were. Ask Hewlett-Packard about the recent resurgence in their minicomputer line—not the 9000, the HP 3000, the machine of the 70s and 80s. Ask IBM about their AS/400 sales—same story. Ask Autodesk about Release 14! It is the hottest seller ever. There's gold in them thar hills.

An Emerging Discipline

Whole product R&D is an emergent discipline. It represents a kind of convergence between high-tech marketing and consumer marketing, where, for the first time, the tools of the latter can be of significant use in solving the problems of the former. Let's look at two examples: focus groups and packaging studies.

As innovation becomes increasingly continuous, focus groups, which are virtually useless in guiding the development of an early market, become effective tools. The reason they are now effective is that the fundamental product proposition is already in the market and absorbed. Until this is the case, consumers are way over their head in trying to anticipate the value and usage of a new high-tech product. But once that proposition is in place, the tool becomes effective. Specifically, it can be used to direct the extension and modification of an existing product line to meet the special needs of a target market segment. In this context, all consumers are asked to do is address relatively minor derivatives from a known entity—something well within their expertise. The information they give back, therefore, is valuable.

Consider another discipline that today is far more advanced in consumer marketing than in high tech—packaging. As an industry, we have considered this to be nothing more than the paint of the box, the logo, the cover. But packaging happens not just on the outside but on the inside, and the goal of good packaging is to ensure a successful experience right out of the box—an area that cries out for more research attention in high tech. Think how many dollars could be diverted into better ends that today go to expensive support services, all because our products are packaged in confusing or obtuse ways.

Now these types of efforts—focus groups and packaging studies—are traditionally located in the marketing department. But in high tech, marketing is too ignorant to drive the bus. What appears to the generalist to be a simple change may in fact cut across some fundamental technology boundary in a radically inappropriate way. Or conversely, what looks impossible to achieve may in fact be a by-product of a minor adjustment. In either case, engineering must be a direct partner in the effort, or it is wasted. It's not market research alone, nor is it just product development. It's whole product R&D, and it implies a new kind of cooperation between organizations traditionally set apart from each other.

Leaving This Book Behind

By way of parting, let us look back over the ground we have covered in this and the previous chapters. We began by isolating a fundamental flaw in the prevailing high-tech marketing model— the notion that rapid mainstream market growth could follow continuously on the heels of early market success. By analyzing the characteristics of visionaries and pragmatists, we were able to see that a far more normal development would be a chasm period of little to no growth. This period was identified as perilous indeed, giving companies every incentive to pass through it as rapidly as possible.

Taking such rapid passage as our charter, we then embarked on setting forth strategy and tactics for accomplishing it. The fundamental strategic principle was to launch a D-Day type of invasion, one focused on a highly specific target segment within a mainstream marketplace. The tactics for implementing that invasion were then set out in four clusters.

To begin with, we had to *target the point of attack,* which meant isolating our target customers and their compelling reason to buy. Then we had to *assemble the invasion force,* constructed around the whole product and the partners and allies needed to make it a reality. The next step was to *define the battle,* by creating our competition and positioning ourselves, in that context, as being easy to buy. Finally, we had to *launch the invasion,* selecting our intended distribution channel and setting our pricing to give us motivational leverage over that channel.

Now we have just spent this last chapter stepping back from the immediate tactics of crossing the chasm, to look at the major commitments that get made in the prechasm phase of an organization's growth, thereby to guard against crippling the success of the postchasm venture. That brings us to the end of this road.

Finally, it should come as no surprise that there are no warranties, expressed or implied, on any of the methods described in this book. You must use them at your own risk. But I do claim that they are the best I know of, and that they are representative of best practices as conducted at The Chasm Group. On behalf of my colleagues there, as well as myself, I wish you the best of success in all your upcoming marketing efforts.

Index

BUSINESS CLASSICS FOR THE INQUISITIVE EXECUTIVE